Preachers and Misfits, Prophets and Thieves

Preachers and Misfits, Prophets and Thieves

The Minister in Southern Fiction

G. Lee Ramsey Jr.

Westminster John Knox Press
LOUISVILLE • LONDON

Scripture quotations are chiefly from the New Revised Standard Version of the Bible, copyright © 1989 by the Division of Christian Education of the National Council of the Churches of Christ in the USA, and used by permission. Those marked RSV are from the Revised Standard Version, copyright 1946, 1952, 1971 by the Division of Christian Education of the National Council of Churches in the USA, and used by permission. KJV, King James Version.

See Permissions, pp. 141–42, for additional permission information. Every effort has been made to determine whether texts are under copyright. If through an oversight any copyrighted material has been used without permission, and the publisher is notified of this, acknowledgment will be made in future printings.

Book design by Drew Stevens
Cover design by designpointinc.com

First edition
Published by Westminster John Knox Press
Louisville, Kentucky

This book is printed on acid-free paper that meets the American National Standards Institute Z39.48 standard. ♾

PRINTED IN THE UNITED STATES OF AMERICA

08 09 10 11 12 13 14 15 16 17 — 10 9 8 7 6 5 4 3 2 1

Library of Congress Cataloging-in-Publication Data

Ramsey, G. Lee.
    Preachers and misfits, prophets and thieves : the minister in southern fiction / G. Lee Ramsey. — 1st ed.
        p. cm.
    Includes bibliographical references and index.
    ISBN 978-0-664-23224-5 (alk. paper)
    1. American fiction—Southern States—History and criticism. 2. Christianity and literature—Southern States—History—20th century. 3. Christianity and literature—Southern States—History—21st century. 4. Clergy in literature. 5. Literature and society—Southern States—History—20th century. 6. Literature and society—Southern States—History—21st century. 7. Stereotypes (Social psychology) in literature. 8. Southern States—In literature. 9. Southern States—Religion. 10. Belief and doubt in literature. 11. Faith in literature. I. Title.

    PS261.R36 2008
    813'.50938228—dc22

                                                                                    2008013186

*For Mary Leslie, Shelley, Luke,
Betty, and Joe*

Could it be that the Lord is here, masquerading behind this simple silly holy face?

—Walker Percy, *The Second Coming*

Contents

Acknowledgments

In the early going on this book, more than one person accused me of dreaming up the ideal project that would allow me to sit around for days on end and read Southern fiction and books about Christian ministry. I may be guilty as charged, but the most gratifying part of the project is that such reading blossomed into fruitful conversations with others about ministry and fiction. My debt to others is great. My hope, now that the book is complete, is that our conversations about Christian ministry and fiction will continue.

I thank my skillful editor at Westminster John Knox Press, Stephanie Egnotovich, who encouraged this effort from day one. She patiently and wisely helped me untangle this book from the brier patch of an overgrown manuscript. Julie Tonini carefully sorted out all the manuscript and production issues necessary to move the project into print.

I received much-needed financial support for this project from the Louisville Institute, and I am sincerely grateful for the confidence of Dr. James W. Lewis, Executive Director, the staff, and the Institute's Board of Directors.

My Academic Dean at Memphis Theological Seminary, Dr. Barbara A. Holmes, and the President of the Seminary, Dr. Daniel Jay Earheart-Brown, have been unfailingly supportive of this project and generous with the resources of the Seminary, including sabbatical time for research and writing.

My teaching colleagues at Memphis Theological Seminary have been a supportive fellowship as I have wound my way through this work. I am especially grateful to the lunch crowd: Professors Barry Bryant, Jeffrey Gros, Virginia Lee, and Matt Matthews. Over numerous sack lunches, they indulged my enthusiasm for the latest discovery of yet another "Southern minister story" and helped me clear the various hurdles I encountered along the way.

A wider circle of friends encouraged me during the unfolding of this project. They provided reading, listening, direction, interest, and support as I sought to connect ministry and fiction. Thank you, Ron Allen, Dale

Andrews, Susan Bond, Chuck Campbell, Cozette Garrett, Ron Johnson, John and Palmer Jones, John and Annie McClure, Mary Alice Mulligan, Teresa Stricklen, Becky Youngblood, and Dawn Ottoni Wilhem.

The professional library staff of MTS has been ever resourceful. Thank you, Steve Edscorn, Jane Williamson, Melissa Hamblin, Mildred Saulsberry, and Susan Stewart.

The selection of stories and reflections upon ministry that eventually found their way into this book first began in a course that I taught to students at Memphis Theological Seminary. These students confirmed my conviction that fiction belongs in theological education. They helped me see the many ways that ministry comes alive when viewed through the lens of story. I am grateful to Victor Adams, Ron Feeser, Regina Hall, Keith Keeton, H. B. Miller, Johnny Parish, Roger Patton, Charles Penson, Ann Phillips, Nick Phillips, Jeff Powell, Joyce Thomas, Kent Wilfong.

In my local congregation, Trinity United Methodist Church in Memphis, I enjoy friendship with a group of fiction readers whose monthly gathering to discuss faith and fiction is a source of delight: Lee Belue, Alicia Le, Carol Raiford, Wendell Stoltz, Libby Streete, Clara Talley, Jamie Windham, and Lois Young. They have read with me several of the stories included herein, and many of their insights about ministry and fiction have enriched my thinking.

Several of the Southern writers whose work appears here graciously consented to meet with me to discuss their work. These are some of the most decent, generous-spirited, and creative individuals whom I have ever met. Conversations with Doris Betts, Clyde Edgerton, Robert Inman, Cassandra King, Dayne Sherman, and Lee Smith fueled my zeal for the topic and reminded me of the mystery that births both art and Christian ministry.

Members of the wider literary guild were helpful as I sought better footing in the world of fiction and ministry, especially regarding the writings of Walker Percy. For their insight, I am thankful to Professors John May of Louisiana State University and John F. Desmond of Whitman College.

During my impressionable high school and college years, several teachers and ministers lit the still-burning fires that illumine Southern fiction and ministry for me. How can I say thanks? With this work, I hope to honor these excellent teachers and ministers. One of them, the late Dr. Floyd Watkins of Emory University, will have to hear my gratitude from the other side. The others—Carolyn Siefferman, Wayne

Brantley, John Kay, Bettie Sellers, and Hamp Watson—I go through my days borrowing your light.

I thank fly fishermen and friends John Buford, Joe Dycus, and Bill Siler, who spent days with me on running water with fishing rods in our hands and the occasional trout dancing at the end of the line, which often renewed my spirit enough to return to the task at hand.

Many other friends grace my days with companionship and creativity. They are present throughout the seasons of life and teach me more about divine love and Christian ministry than this or any other book could ever contain. If I never make another friend in this world, I have already received a second helping in Allen and Marcia Craig, Jeff and Kathy Irwin, Virginia Lee, Don and Sherry Park, Joe and Betty Reiff, and Billy and Joni Laney Vaughan.

Finally, there is the constant affirmation of my parents, Gilbert and Frances Ramsey, and the unparalleled love of my immediate family, Mary Leslie, Shelley, and Luke. They know every story in the book; they make faith and fiction complete.

Introduction

It was pretty ornery preaching—all about brotherly love, and such-like
tiresomeness; but everybody said it was a good sermon. . . . It did seem
to me to be one of the roughest Sundays I had run across yet.
—*Huckleberry Finn*

At least since Mark Twain gave us the earthy commentary of Huckleberry Finn, the Southern writer has applauded, scrutinized, satirized,
lampooned, sentimentalized, and generally worked over the public figure of the minister. From the preacher who delivers a fiery sermon (a
"scaldabanco," they used to call such exhorters) to the pastor who counsels with a troubled teenager, from a backwoods religious misfit pro-
nouncing doom upon a Sodom of the South to a self-serving charlatan
hiding behind the clerical collar, a grab bag of images of the minister
falls open, and preachers and misfits, prophets and thieves, all come
popping out.

If you think ministry is dull, the notion did not come from fiction,
at least not *Southern* fiction. The colorful assortment of ministers in
contemporary Southern fiction springs from the deeply rooted yet
kudzu-like presence of religion—Protestant and Catholic—across the
Southern landscape. Snake-handling ministers, though diminishing,
are still around. On the same city block of almost any Southern city of
a hundred thousand persons or more, you are apt to find genteel Episcopalians worshiping in an exquisite neo-Gothic sanctuary that shares
real-estate boundaries with a storefront church of hallelujah-shouting,
hand-clapping neo-Pentecostals. The fry cook at the local Southern
restaurant, as in William Price Fox's short story "Southern Fried," is just
as likely to be a part-time preacher who reads Immanuel Kant on his
breaks as he is to be a Holy Roller. In the Southern way of religious life,
this all makes perfectly good sense.[1]

Yet for all the ministers who hold forth in contemporary Southern fiction, rarely do we turn to fiction as a means to understand the ministry,
the Christian congregation, and the church within the community. This

is unfortunate, given that the Southern region of the United States, a region that Flannery O'Connor once described as "Christ haunted," is particularly fertile soil for both religion and fiction. Indeed, Southern fiction writers are among the sharpest yet most underrecognized observers of the ministry and the Christian church today.[2]

This book focuses on how Southern writers picture the ministry and how such fictional pictures cast light upon our understanding of the Christian ministry in its various offices.

Many of the fictional Southern ministers we are about to meet are edgy characters. Like Barry Hannah's Rev. Byron Egan in *Yonder Stands Your Orphan*, they are zany and bent out of shape when compared to conventional ministers of the Protestant mainstream. Some of them are mystics or misfits, like Lee Smith's Rev. Virgil Shepherd in *Saving Grace* or Flannery O'Connor's Hazel Motes in *Wise Blood*. Some haunt the margins of Southern life, whether in our shining "New South" cities or traditional rural crossroads, while preaching a gospel that startles and compels. Some of these ministers you will want to invite home for dinner, and others you will want to show the highway. Often their oddness is part of their appeal. But it is also part of their gift. They come at us with such colorful force that they challenge us to think about the church and ministry in new ways. They shock us with their convictions *and* their deceptions. After meeting these fictional ministers, we can't help but ask ourselves what really matters in Christian ministry today? Can they help us reimagine ministry in ways that will bring new life to church and community?

Hearing them preach and pray, watching them counsel and cajole, seeing them buckle under or rise above moral temptation—all this just about forces us to examine questions of responsibility that clergy face in the early twenty-first century. How to minister is particularly vexing now within a changing South where old and new, black and white, Hispanic and Asian, religious and secular, Democrat and Republican, rural and urban cannot help but meet, collide, sometimes explode, and occasionally reconcile. With these lively ministers as companions, we can puzzle out what leads to fulfillment or collapse of pastoral leadership. Fiction, like Scripture, can "read us." Fiction can name, identify, clarify, and confound what it means to be Christian ministers or laity in the modern/postmodern era. These fictional ministers can help us question and refine our own theology, self-understanding, moral practices, and approaches to pastoral ministry and the Christian life.

The scope of the book is limited to Christian clergy—Protestant and to a lesser extent Catholic, a minority religious body in the South but with major literary voices—because these figures are far and away the most prevalent in the fiction of the region, a region that religious historians repeatedly characterize as predominantly "conservative, Protestant evangelical." In this sense, the fiction does imitate the reality of the culture.[3]

If you happen to be a Southerner, particularly a Southerner interested in ministry, you will find here stories and characters that shine the spotlight upon your own religious and cultural experience. Some of the characters discussed here may cause you to ask yourself if there is anything you want to do in light of what you have read. If you happen not to be a Southerner, you have the safe advantage of being able to observe ministry in the South without then being held directly accountable for what you have seen. Then again, given that conservative, Protestant evangelicalism, the religion of the South, has now been exported within the United States to the point of saturating the religious market, you may not be safe at all. As the Southern fiction scholar Fred Hobson says, "Dixie has to some extent become Americanized, but America has absorbed much of Dixie too. Country music, fried chicken, stock car racing, evangelical religion, and opposition to busing schoolchildren— all these have replaced cotton as Dixie's leading export." And as writer John Egerton presciently observed in the early 1970s, "The North has lately shown itself to be more and more like the South in the political, racial, social, and religious inclinations of its collective majority." In that case, for non-Southerners, what you discover in these novels and short stories may surprisingly echo some of the expressions of ministry that you find today on street corners and in sanctuaries in places as distant from the South as Lansing, Michigan, and Seattle, Washington. You can decide.[4]

The fiction I explore here is *contemporary Southern fiction.* But the category of *contemporary fiction* is a loose and broad one. In this case, it refers to novels or short stories written either in the twentieth or early twenty-first century. Admittedly, this is a wide time spectrum. It would be foolhardy for me to review such a vast period of literature if this were an academic project directed toward literary scholars and English departments. That would require a much closer analysis of author, text, and context of each work than I am capable of, and it would force greater critical precision and restraint. But that is not what I intend.

Rather, I embark here upon a freewheeling survey of regional Southern fiction written over roughly the past one hundred years. I have followed my nose and the signposts of friends and fiction writers to some of the better and lesser known novels and short stories in which ministers appear. Then I try to listen to what these fictional ministers say about ministry and the church of the South. I am not seeking a monochromatic image of the minister in Southern literature as much as a *variety of images* of clergy that can open up fruitful discussions about Christian ministry. With this approach I assume that, though dated, the Southern writers of the earlier and middle periods of the twentieth century—Hurston, Ellison, and O'Connor—have as much to say about the church and the ministry of the South as the more recent arrivals to the Southern literary scene. In fact, given that Southern literature has always grappled with what Louis Rubin calls "the impossible load of the past," earlier fictional characterizations of ministers provide one way to think about the changing yet enduring nature of Christian ministry in the South.[5]

As a devoted reader of Southern literature *and* an ordained minister, I bring together here two lifelong commitments that help define who I am. A great deal of how I see the world and my place in it, particularly as a professing Christian in the South, and even how I read the literature of the region, grows out of my own upbringing as the son of a Methodist clergyman in the South, a vocation that eventually, after my share of struggling with the "preacher's kid syndrome," became my own. I know ministry from the inside out. Over the past twenty-five years I have regularly stood in pulpits and beside hospital beds and now in the classroom of a theological seminary. Most of what I have learned and shared with others both as a United Methodist and a Christian boils down to grace in its many forms, but that doesn't stop me from wanting to understand.

But I also speak of literature and ministry *as a Southerner*, reared across the piney woods and coastal plains of South Georgia and residing now upon the bluffs of Memphis and within walking distance of James Cobb's evocatively named "the most Southern place on earth," the Mississippi Delta. My college English professor, the late Dr. Floyd Watkins of Emory University, a Southern literature scholar and straight-talking Presbyterian, stoked the fires of my interest in Faulkner, O'Connor, Penn Warren, Hurston, Welty, and those writers who have followed. He helped me see that to read them and others like them—as a Southerner—is in part an exercise in self and regional identification that provides a place to stand, and as Eudora Welty said, "It is by knowing where you stand that you grow able to judge where you are." Ralph Ellison's protagonist in *Invisible Man* says, "To lose a sense of *where* you are implies the danger of losing a sense of *who* you are." To be "from somewhere" and to know it, and to know one's place within that culture, then makes it possible to see and know others more fully. The obverse is also true, as Flannery O'Connor wryly remarked when viewing a rack of mass-market books: "You know what's the matter with them? They're not from anywhere."[6]

I take for granted that there is a literature of the South, black and white, and now the beginnings of a Hispanic and Asian Southern Literature, whether every university literature department agrees or not. For this study, by "Southern Literature" I mean the novels and short stories of writers who either originated in the geographical South and claim its mark upon their work or who consciously and over time have identified themselves with the region, its culture, its history, and its fiction. The geography is roughly delineated by those states located south of the Mason and Dixon line, including parts of Maryland and pushing the boundaries a little to Oklahoma and Arkansas. Whether all the writers included here *should* be categorized as Southern writers in the strictest academic sense, I will leave to the wisdom of the literary critics, citing the waxing and waning of the debate on the Southernness of Mark Twain as an ambiguous case in point.[7]

All the novels and short stories included here are Southern in the broad sense that I intend and that I think would be readily accepted by the general reader. Some have more lasting literary value than others, but each of them speaks to the matter of ministry in the region. Because these Southern authors so frequently include ministers in their work, they are a good bunch to listen to. They speak creatively not only to those of us who are Christian believers in the South, but also to anyone else who wants to think imaginatively about ministry in the Southern region of the United States.

The book begins by listening to several fictional ministers as they talk about the *vocation* of the minister. The matter of religious "call" is central to the identity and work of the Christian minister. Distinctive notions of call emerge in Southern fiction, from conversion or crisis experience that leads to "call," to institutional pressure or family expectation. Some ministers are highly conflicted spiritually and emotionally about their vocations; others probably should be but are not. These fictional ministers cast light upon the uniqueness of the religious calling and the responsibilities that ordained ministers face.

Each succeeding chapter explores either an office or dominant image of the minister through fictional ministers in Southern novels or short stories. While Christian ministry cannot be limited to just one office or image, by looking at each of them separately, we can see more deeply into the ministry as a whole. Chapters view the minister as (2) *preacher,* (3) *evangelist,* (4) *pastor,* (5) *priest,* (6) *con man and thief,* (7) *church politician,* (8) *prophet,* (9) *mystic and misfit,* and (10) *community person.* Within each chapter, we will hear what these compelling fictional ministers have to say to us about ministry and its various offices and images, especially as we understand it within the churches and communities of the South.

Throughout our visits with these spirited ministers, I also pay attention to clergy character within community. What beliefs and values actually motivate these characters? We meet cutthroat minister politicians like Rev. Roger Hagan in Will Campbell's *The Convention,* and we come to know ministers who wrestle honestly with the moral ambiguities of ministry such as Rev. Joel King in Martin Clark's *Plain Heathen Mischief.* Are the actions of the fictional ministers consistent with their professed beliefs and consistent with theologically sound understandings of their office? Why or why not? What can we learn from these characters, such as Gail Godwin's Rev. Margaret Bonner in *Evensong,* about pastoral practices that we could not have learned otherwise? How might such understandings deepen our own faithfulness and effectiveness in pastoral ministry? What makes for a "good" or "excellent" pastor in terms of moral decision making, care for others in the name of Christ, and execution of leadership within the church and community? What notable insights do the fictional ministers (and their authors) offer to help steer clergy and congregations forward in religious life today? In what ways do the fictional ministers show us the stumbling blocks to faithful ministry?

Readers who sit for awhile with these sometimes quirky and thoroughly human ministers of Southern fiction will be given new eyes to see the ministry and the church within Southern culture. They will become acquainted with some new, if fictional, friends who often say something worth hearing. As one of my students who is an ordained minister said after meeting Rev. Joe Pike Moseley in Robert Inman's *Dairy Queen Days,* "I wish I knew a Joe Pike Moseley that I could sit down and talk to." To which I replied, "You do."

1

Whose Voice Is That?

The Vocation of the Minister and Southern Fiction

> My ordination was in this church. You were just a baby. And I preached
> a sermon, sort of a call to arms, about the Disciples going out to witness.
> "Go ye unto all the world . . ." Young preachers tend to be full of piss
> and vinegar.
> —Rev. Joe Pike Moseley in Robert Inman's *Dairy Queen Days*

> He simply grew up certain that it would be so—that he would be a
> preacher. Not because of any belief he could actually pin down. Instead,
> it was because of a powerful lifelong desire that there be "something else."
> —Dr. Swain Hammond in Peggy Payne's *Revelation*

When you read just about any piece of Southern fiction written over the
past one hundred years, there is at least half a chance that you will find
a minister tucked somewhere within its pages. The ordained minister
shows up in stories as both an individual person and as a *called* representative of something much larger: God, the church, Christian tradition, and religious experience.

The word vocation signifies that the minister is "called out." While
God calls all believers to faithfulness, the call of the ordained minister
singles the hearer out for representative ministries of the congregation.
The call establishes that this particular Christian has received certain
gifts (charisms)—such as preaching, presiding in worship, consecrating
the sacraments, and organizing the church—that are for the good of the
whole. God bestows these gifts upon the minister to edify the body
(Ephesians 4:12). Among the laity, some may even share these same
gifts, but the pastor is designated to be the "official" bearer of these gifts
for the whole church. As William Willimon puts it, "The difference
between a pastor who visits, preaches, and baptizes, and any other
skilled layperson who performs these same functions is in the pastor's
officialness." In this representative sense, the call of the ordained minister is unique.[1]

No question is more vexing for the minister and more inviting of the
novelist's exploration than this: What does it mean to be "called" by
God? This is the question that starts all ministers down the path toward

ordination. Just as their counterparts in real life, the ministers of Southern fiction wrestle—sometimes openly and sometimes in secret—with questions of calling: Who am I? What is my purpose? What difference does my calling make in the way that I live? As Barbara Brown Taylor notes, "When God calls, people respond in a variety of ways. Some pursue ordination and others put pillows over their heads, but the vast majority seeks to answer God by changing how they live their more or less ordinary lives."[2]

So, how does "call" come to a person? Call occurs in many ways, as Southern fiction helps us to see. The call to ministry is often complex and mysterious. A close brush with the holy often shows up in the call of ministers, like Moses hearing the voice of God and seeing the burning bush or the speech-stopping angel who confronts Zechariah (Exodus 3; Luke 1:5–23). But call also comes to the minister through the church, family, and the experience of salvation. How does the minister know if he or she is being called? This is the first question we ask of our fictional ministers, whose answers lead us into our exploration of the Christian ministry.

Called by the Voice of God

It is nothing if not biblical that the vocation of the minister is associated with sound. Ministers speak of "being called," or "called out." In Scripture, God *calls* to Adam and Eve in the cool of the garden (Genesis 3:9). Samuel *hears* the voice of God in the stillness of the temple (1 Samuel 3:3–14). In one of the paradigmatic call scenes within Hebrew Scripture, Isaiah hears God say, "Whom shall I send and who will go for us?" (Isaiah 6:8). Later the voice of God identifies Jesus at his baptism as the "Beloved" Son (Mark 1:11) and at the transfiguration tells Jesus' followers, "Listen to him" (Mark 9:7). Whether it comes as a roar or a whisper, heard by the solitary person at prayer or gathered with the congregation, believers acknowledge hearing the sound and sometimes the distinctive words of God's voice.

Many Southern believers associate religious experience with sound. As Charles Reagan Wilson says, "Southern Evangelicalism prizes religious experience, and its characteristic experiential orientation is toward sound. It is a religion of the word." And the fiction writer Doris Betts recalls, "In my church, words and The Word were almost sub-sacraments themselves, could work wonders, could transubstantiate any old thing by the side of a red-clay road." When the minister says that she has been "called," she then attempts to explain to others—friends, family, congregations, boards of ministry—what or who she has heard.[3]

The problem is that the minister and those around him often stand on shaky ground when it comes to discerning if what the minister has heard is actually the voice of God. For example, the Southern Baptist, Jayber, in Wendell Berry's novel *Jayber Crow*, thinks that he might be called, but he isn't sure. Even after he decides that God has not actually spoken to him, Jayber cannot shake the haunting possibility that he may have been wrong:

> Though I knew that actually I had heard no voice, I could not dismiss the possibility that it had spoken and I had failed to hear it because of some deficiency in me or something wrong that I had done. My fearful uncertainty lasted for months. Finally, I reasoned that in dealing with God you had better give Him the benefit of the doubt. I decided that I had better accept the call that had not come, just in case it had come and I had missed it.

God's call is frightfully difficult to determine. It is always possible to be listening to the wrong voice or to misunderstand what one has heard.[4]

North Carolinian Peggy Payne's novel *Revelation* takes up this question of discerning God's voice. Dr. Swain Hammond, minister of the liberal, university-based Westside Presbyterian Church in Chapel Hill, North Carolina, is cooking pork and green peppers on a charcoal grill when he thinks that he hears the voice of God speaking directly to him.

> The sound comes up over the hill. He stands frozen and feels it coming. One quick cut. Like a hugely amplified PA system, blocks away, switched on for a moment by mistake ". . . Know that truth is . . ." There is no mistaking the voice. At the first sound, the first rolling syllable, he's swimming up out of a sleep, shocked into wakefulness. He stands where he stood, feeling all through him the murmuring life of each of his million cells.

When the sound recedes, Hammond walks back to his wife, Julie, and grabs her tightly, pulling her close to him.

> "What happened?" she says. She wants to shake him. Why won't he say? "Are you okay?" He tries to say it: "Julie, I heard God." But it won't come out . . . "I don't know how to tell you. You'll think I'm crazy."

Indeed, many in Hammond's congregation do think he is crazy when he tells them that he has literally heard the voice of God. One church member tries to explain things to him: "People just don't understand. It's—people are frightened of what might be happening to you." Another member of the congregation who has been sent by the church elders to talk to Hammond says,

> "Look Swain, what it is, I'd have to say that, well, people were . . . concerned for you. That's all. You've always had everything under control, very well organized, had your head on straight is what I'm trying to say. Everybody's always admired that. So it's a surprise—all this. That's what people were saying."

Ironically, while Hammond feels more assured than ever of his call to ministry, the more he insists upon the truthfulness of his experience, the more the congregation pulls away from him. His personal, inward, and mystical experience of divine calling unsettles the ordered, rational religion of the educated, Reformed congregation.[5]

Hammond's predicament reflects the rough seam in Southern religious life where experiential faith (religion of the heart, it is usually called) meets reasonable religion (religion of the head). This is a historical divide that can be traced back in American religious history to the eighteenth and nineteenth centuries and the First and Second Great Awakenings. It is true that these revivals and the resulting collision between pietism and rationalism played a huge part in turning Southern Christianity toward a preference for emotional expressiveness in worship and Christian life. Yet pietism never wiped out the intellectual capital of the Southern church as a whole or the preference of many of its adherents for faith served by reason.[6]

This tension between head and heart helps us understand Hammond's struggles to communicate his experience. Hearing for the first time what he believes to be the voice of God, Hammond is separated from the congregation by his inability to communicate the experience and their unwillingness to receive it. His efforts are not successful, so he becomes isolated from his congregation and then discouraged about his vocation. In the end, he is forced to resign from his congregation.

Discerning one's call to ministry often plunges a person into turbulent vocational waters. Like Hammond, the contemporary pastor often wonders if his or her inward perception of God's call is genuine or a manifestation of a personal psychological need. Is Swain Hammond newly empowered by fresh religious perception of God's voice, or is he simply talking to himself?

The minister who relies solely upon the inward experience of calling, and such ministers crop up all over the South, is in a dangerous position. He has no checks from within the community. The pastor who is a representative of the church as the body of Christ is never a sole operator for the Divine. A pastor must be authorized by something much more important than private needs and perceptions. Though personally moving, moments of inward religious revelation require the external validation of other voices.

These other voices, sometimes echoing and other times obscuring the sounds of God, come from a variety of sources: the church, the family, and the wider community. To discern if God is truly calling, the hearer must listen to each of these voices, often simultaneously.

Call and the Voice of the Church

The church is one of the most theologically and historically significant voices that calls the believer to Christian ministry. Through the congregation the minister discerns a call from God, and within the congregation the minister works out that call from God. Most ministers preach and pray within a congregation whose members "help" the minister flesh out her call—daily. As Tom Long puts it, "It is easy to forget that we come *from* these people not *to* them from outside. We are not visitors from clergy-land, strangers from an unknown land, ambassadors from seminary-land. . . . We are members of the body of Christ, commissioned to preach by the very people to whom we are about to speak." Ministers emerge from among the *laos*, the people of God, who are the living witness to Jesus' promise that "where two or three are gathered in my name, I am there among them" (Matthew 18:20).[7]

Ordination is meaningless without a congregation or specific community in which to work out one's calling "with fear and trembling," as the apostle Paul puts it (Philippians 2:12). In Mississippi native Richard Wright's "Fire and Cloud," set in the early 1930s during the Jim Crow days, Rev. Taylor struggles with the tension between his own personal call and the voice of the congregation. He vacillates between understanding his call primarily for the purpose of individual evangelism and the recognition that his African American congregation is calling for someone to help deliver them from racist oppression. Taylor finally sees that his call cannot be separated from the social needs of his own people. He jubilantly surrenders to the voice of God speaking through the community.

> Then the crowd began to slow, barely moving. Taylor looked ahead and wondered what was about to happen; he wondered without fear; as though whatever would or could happen could not hurt this many-limbed, many legged, many-handed crowd that was he.[8]

Rev. Taylor finally recognizes that he is both a servant of God and a servant of the people. The call from God is a call to deeper response to the congregation and their hunger for faithful leadership.

But the church in general and congregations in particular always tax the faith of the minister. Given that the hypocrisy, halfheartedness, pettiness, and self-interest that goes on everywhere else is just as easily found within the church, ministers will always be tempted to cast around for more hospitable ground in which to sow the gospel. Precisely because the South as a whole claims to be so devout, the foibles of the congregation can lead the ordained minister to cynicism or disillusionment. H. L. Mencken's barbed satire of the South as "a cesspool of Baptists, a miasma of Methodists, snake-charmers, phony real estate operators, and syphilitic evangelists" stings all the more because the devout firmly believe that true faith should elevate its adherents. So anyone who thinks that God may be calling needs to take a hard look at the congregation and make sure that, when all is said and done, he or she believes that God can speak through such a flawed vessel. For as Wesley Benefield says to Miss Mattie in Clyde Edgerton's *Killer Diller* when she encourages him to become a preacher, "I don't know. I'd have to get ordained. I'm not sure I'd like the ordainers."[9]

The Christian congregation is so flawed because it is composed of real people who, as Martin Luther established, are simultaneously sinners and justified. The congregation and the minister may be on their way to sanctification, but few (if any) have arrived yet. Thank God that believers do not have to bear the burden of striving after self-made perfection. Grace abounds. Only the pastor who knows the extravagance of God's grace can fully surrender to the call to serve among the stiffnecked yet caring people who comprise the church.

Call and the Voice of Family

Often intertwined with the voice of the church in the South is the voice of the family, a persistent external voice that calls to the minister, either in sound or silence. Some ministers hear their call as a continuation of a devout family's spiritual heritage. Others hear their call because of the family's rejection of belief. Either way, because of the linkage of religion and family in the South, those who hear a call from God often listen to it filtered through the prayers and shouts, the jokes and warnings and instructions of the family. Even those who decide that God is not calling them into ministry often do so in response to the sounds of family and faith.

Children of the clergy especially wrestle with family and call. Sons and daughters of ministers may not be predestined to enter the ministry, but in the South most preachers' kids struggle with a religious vocation at one time or another that can seem almost foreordained. Some of them follow naturally in these vocational footprints to the third or fourth generation.

In *Mammoth Cheese*, by the Virginia writer Sheri Holman, Pastor Leland Vaughan is the rector of St. Barnabas Episcopal Church, in Three Chimneys, Virginia. The family pictures in the parsonage hallway are daily reminders to Vaughan that his call to ministry comes within a long line of clergy.

> There was no one in the hallway but Leland and the Wall of Ancestors . . . two hundred years' worth of framed uncles and aunts, fourth and fifth cousins, men muttonchopped and mustachioed, women with stern Depression-era finger waves. . . . He would have thought a family made up predominantly of clergy would have shrunk from the vainglory of personal iconography, but his seemed to relish it. . . . This church had been the mainstay and life's work of every man on that wall.

In his acceptance of the ministry as a family inheritance, Vaughan preserves family religious tradition and tries to assure that the Christian tradition within the Southern community will go forward even in the face of the emerging forces of the "New South" that erode traditional commitments like family and faith. With the support of his religious inheritance, Leland Vaughn preaches, administers the sacraments, prays, counsels, and presides over community affairs in a changing Southern township as if the future of everyone depends upon him.[10]

This passing of the ministerial mantle from parent to child is common in many branches of Southern Protestantism. For example, senior Baptist preachers frequently bequeath "their congregations" to a son or daughter who has been apprenticing for full leadership. The Rev. Martin

Luther King Sr. and Rev. Billy Graham both come to mind as ministers who have handed on their congregations and ministries to the next generation. In United Methodist conferences, extended ministerial families and kinship networks sometimes dominate the denominational affairs of a state or region. Many Pentecostal congregations and denominations are "family led." These family dynamics are certainly not limited to the South, but the situation occurs so frequently there as to be distinctive.

At the same time, the pressure cooker of some Southern religious families can drive a son or daughter away from a religious vocation. By their rejections of faith, some ministers' children show just how strong family vocational expectations can be. The variety of rebellious sons and daughters of ministers in Southern fiction illumines the pressure that these children experience to conform to unrealistic familial and community expectations. For example, in Georgian Ferrol Sams's *The Whisper of the River*, Vashti, the daughter of a prominent Baptist minister in Macon, Georgia, expertly ushers the college-age protagonist, Porter, into full sexual knowledge. She explains her casual attitude toward sex with a stinging rebuke of her father: "Because my daddy's a preacher and a phony." In Vashti's case, her religious family's hypocritical expectation of conformity is the very thing that drives her away from faith.[11]

The public scrutiny of ministers' children who live in a religious and social fishbowl and the pressure of family and congregation to press them into a specific and preordained social mold creates resentment and loneliness for those children. Trout Moseley, the confused yet determined sixteen-year-old protagonist of Robert Inman's *Dairy Queen Days*, speaks for many of them: "He was quite sick of all this goodness, but he felt trapped. . . . He was still a preacher's kid and that carried a certain aloneness to it."[12]

If such a child of the minister finally hears his or her own call to the ministry, and many do, it takes time and distance from the family to sort out the confusing sounds of family expectations and God's call. When she does, it comes as a great yet fulfilling surprise to discover that the very God and family traditions that she has rejected have come home in a new way. Those rebellious sons and daughters who run far and fast sometimes run straight into the arms of God. Their stories recapitulate the Old Testament drama of Isaac, Jacob, and Esau and the New Testament parable of the Prodigal Son (Genesis 32:28; Luke 15:24).

Southern writers echo this theme in stories in which ministers' children wander far from their spiritual homes yet finally arrive at a place

of mature acceptance of their calling, if not always as ministers themselves, then as recipients of the family's gift of faith. For example, Sandra Hollins Flowers's short story "Hope of Zion" features an African
American minister, Rev. Douglas Fairfax, who prepares to "hand over"
his congregation to his daughter, Veronica, even though she does not
want to assume the responsibility. She returns to the annual homecoming service to tell her father that once and for all she is leaving behind
his dream for her. But in the exuberant worship service that concludes
the story, Veronica Fairfax "gets happy" and claims her birthright.[13]

There is yet another way that Southern families contribute to the calling of ministers. Some use a religious calling to *avoid* or defy family
expectations. We find a situation like this in Robert Inman's *Dairy Queen
Days*. Rev. Joe Pike Moseley becomes a Methodist minister to escape the
expectation of his stern father, Leland, that Joe would manage the family textile mill in the small Georgia town of Moseley. Family expectation
that Joe will run the mill is so high that ministry is one of his only
"respectable" alternatives. But his evasion catches up with him and
throws Joe into a severe vocational and identity crisis that comes to a
head on Easter Sunday, when he walks out of worship, apologizing to his
congregation, "I'm sorry. I've got to go." Whereupon he jumps on a
reconditioned Triumph motorcycle and rides off to College Station,
Texas, to look for the ghost of his former self and the glory days of playing college football with the legendary Bear Bryant at Texas A&M (and
who could be more revered in Southern civil religion than Bear Bryant?).
Joe Pike's Easter Sunday congregation watches in "a long fascinated
silence, a great holding of breath," as their minister comes unglued.[14]

Joe Pike's crisis stems from his inability to distinguish between the
voice of family and the voice of God. As his wife, Irene, explains, "I
think he had God and Leland Moseley confused. He wanted to please
Leland, but he couldn't bring himself to go to the mill. So he turned to
God, and Leland couldn't argue much with that. Only later, he began
to figure out that he turned to God for the wrong reasons." Joe Pike tries
to come to grips with how family and religious tradition lead to such
turbulence in life and ministry. The demanding voice of family drives
Joe Pike toward ministry for the wrong reasons, which creates a whole
heap of vocational uncertainty for him and pain for those around him.[15]

Nevertheless, the impact of family upon ministerial calling in the
South is powerful but not necessarily determinative. Christian commitment lives toward the future where opposites—slaves and free, male and
female, Jews and Greeks, parents and children—will be reconciled

(Galatians 3:28). In the light of family, a Veronica Fairfax or Joe Pike Moseley may question their own motives for ministry and find those motives less than pure. Such self-scrutiny may lead the minister away from ordination, as in Joe Pike Moseley's case, or as in Veronica Fairfax's case, to embrace her calling, where amid the ambiguities of faith she knows that "Jesus will make a way." Through doubt, struggle with God, family, and the congregation, such ministers emerge to affirm a vocation that is bigger than oneself and one's own family.[16]

Salvation and Calling

For many ministers in the South, calling is directly tied to their own experiences of salvation. For example, in Bobbie Ann Mason's short story "The Retreat," Georgeann is married to Rev. Shelby Pickett. Part-time pastor of Grace United Methodist Church in western Kentucky, Pickett is also a full-time electrician because in his small church "the pay is too low." Georgeanne's mother is suspicious of Pickett's call to ministry and warns her daughter: "Delinquents who suddenly get saved make the worst kind of preachers—just like former drug addicts in their zealousness." The mother's rebuke may be too severe, but she knows to keep an eye upon a minister whose call to the ministry follows close on the heels of a sudden conversion.[17]

This well-worn pattern of conversion and call runs straight through the Christian tradition. From Paul's blinding Damascus Road conversion (Acts 9) to the beckoning call of St. Augustine through the voice of a child, "Take and read, take and read," Christians who have suddenly seen the light of salvation have frequently heard the call to tell the story. This evangelical impulse has had deep roots in Southern religious soil at least since the Great Revival of the early nineteenth century, when the experience of personal salvation became the defining mark of genuine faith. Southern writers have to look no further than around the corner or down the road to find a live specimen of conservative evangelicalism whose preachers willingly testify to their own conversions while exhorting their hearers to the same. Southern fiction has parodied the character ad nauseum. But the real thing continues to happen as the wayward sinner of the South comes to Jesus in a moment of heartfelt contrition and then surrenders to "the call."

A quick look at the raucous variety of ministers in the South, real and imagined, can easily lead one to conclude that God will use just about any willing vessel to get across the good news of redemption. Snatched from Satan's snares, or slowly drawn into the forgiving light of Christ, many of the ministers of the South sing the evangelical national anthem, "Amazing Grace, How Sweet the Sound," to tell their own story of call and redemption.[18]

Many Sounds, One Call

This variety of voices—the inner voice of God, church, family, salvation—might give the impression that the call to Christian ministry is hopelessly cacophonous. With all of these distinctive sounds, and none of them pure because tainted with sin, how could anyone claim to "know" that God has spoken? The motives of ministers are outrageously mixed and frequently confusing. In Horton Davies's phrase, many ministers do appear to be "divines in doubt" as they stumble forward in faith. We should not be surprised when, in Robert Inman's *Dairy Queen Days*, young Trout presses his dad to explain why he's a minister, Joe Pike answers, "Hmmm? Let me sleep on that one?" No matter how robustly the minister may sing "Blessed Assurance, Jesus Is Mine," it often masks inward confusion about one's call. As Rev. Swain Hammond worries in Peggy Payne's *Revelation*, maybe the only call he really hears is the sound of his own need.[19]

Yet to turn away from the call of ministry because the sounds are frequently discordant is a grave theological mistake. The call to Christian ministry surely is ambiguous, and even more so the fulfillment of it. As Doris Betts says about the work of Christian ministry, "It is terribly hard; I don't know how they do it." Preachers whom God calls to trumpet the resurrection of Christ often emit the pitiful sounds of human whining. Pastors who should offer a hearty meal of the bread of life regularly serve little more than crumbs of pious platitudes. As Robert Inman says, "Ministers are just as human as everyone else. I would expect them to have questions about their calling just like the rest of us." Through flawed yet realistic ministers, writers like Inman remind us of the biblical foundation of all Christian faithfulness: "We have this treasure in clay jars" (2 Corinthians 4:7). The motives of ministers are mixed because this side of death and whatever follows, ministers cannot (and should not, theologically speaking) shed their skin, their humanity.[20]

The Catholic Church first understood the paradoxical nature of Christian ministry. Fallible humans, hopelessly flawed but for the saving grace of God, still communicate the presence of the Divine. Beginning with Augustine's controversy with the Donatists and culminating in the Council of Trent, Catholicism carved out a doctrine that points like a compass to the true north of God as the beginning and end of all Christian grace. Finally, whether the priest or preacher soars like a red-tailed hawk or crawls like a garden slug does not change one bit the nature of God or the validity of the sacraments that the priest administers. God does not, in the end, depend upon the ministers' or the laity's moral perfection, intelligence, competence, sensitivity, or leadership ability, to name just a few of the traits that congregations expect ministers to possess.

It could be that Protestant ministers who doubt their call to ministry because of their own mixed motives are neither Catholic nor Protestant enough. Among Protestants, Luther should have put to rest any notion that the Christian believer could ever be spiritually *worthy* of their calling. In Luther's formulation, we are "simultaneously sinners yet justified." This goes as much for the ordained minister as for the laity. Ministers who think that ordination should erase the fault lines of sin have not taken Luther or Calvin, that detective of depravity, to heart. Yes, ordination entails a moral watchfulness and the social expectation that the minister will try to lead a life full of "fruit of the Spirit" (Galatians 5:22–23). Character does matter. But striving for sanctification on the part of the minister, a particularly Wesleyan emphasis, only makes sense in light of one's own recognition of sinfulness. Theologically speaking, real saints are more human, not less, more aware of and accepting of their own humanity, sinful yet redeemed by the mercy of God. If the Southern writer seems particularly prone to pluck at the fraying threads of sin in the minister's robe, perhaps they do the ministry a service. They remind ministers that their calling is not to become a super-starched saint. Rather, the minister represents what it means to be a human being in the eyes of God, forever and always a sinner, yet saved.

In the end, all of the sounds that beckon certain human beings to respond as Samuel did—"Speak, for your servant is listening" (1 Samuel 3:10)—lead toward one call, varied though its expressions may be. Whether hearing the sound through family or church or a particularly intense experience of conversion, the impression of God is audible enough to make the hearer sit up and take notice. What arrests the listener is that in the sound is a purpose, a call: "Go, tell." "Feed my sheep." "Prepare a table." "Bind up the wounds." "Welcome the prodigal."

Discernment of the Voice is complex and often confusing. Sadly, some ministers discover that they were listening to the wrong sounds; others, that the voice they once heard has stopped calling. Great pain or betrayal can follow, which is why the individual call of the minister always needs to be confirmed by the wider community. According to Jesus in Matthew's Gospel, "Not everyone who says to me, 'Lord, Lord,' will enter the kingdom of heaven" (7:21). And some who say, "Here am I; send me," are not hearing well (Isaiah 6:8).

But for those whom God does call and equips for ordained Christian ministry, there are "varieties of gifts, but the same Spirit" (1 Corinthians 12:4). God showers gifts upon the whole people (the *laos*), and to some, the ordained minister, God issues a call to serve the whole people by using these gifts in a representative ministry that edifies the church (Ephesians 4:11–12). The ordained is yoked to God and the congregation by this vocation.

Ministers live out the call by offering their gifts through a particular set of practices and responsibilities: to preach, preside over the worship service, extend pastoral care, lead the church in the march for justice, and administer the life of the congregation. These are the core "offices" of ministers that shape their days. These offices help to identify "the minister" within the community. In fact, from one Christian congregation to another, depending upon denominational tradition and congregational context, the term that the congregation uses to designate the minister indicates which of the ministry offices the congregation especially values. One congregation may call its minister "Preacher" while another will call him "Brother" (which suggests the community role of ministry), and yet another will call their minister "Pastor," or within Catholicism, "Father."

When writers of the South create stories about ministers, they usually accent one or more of these vocational offices, such as the minister as preacher, pastor, or evangelist. Reviewed individually over the next several chapters through the various offices of ministry, these ministers present a varied image of the one whom God calls to minister in the name of Jesus Christ. If we will let them, these fictional ministers can challenge and enliven our own ministries. After all, writers, readers, and ministers, as Allan Gurganus suggests, respond to a similar calling: to become part of "a story that's larger than ourselves."[21]

2

Riding the Word

The Minister as Preacher

And the Master said, . . . "Hickman, Rise up on the Word and ride. All time is mine. . . . Just be prepared. Now get up there and ride!"
—Rev. Alonzo Hickman in Ralph Ellison's *Juneteenth*

His was a voice able to penetrate the latched, inner iron gate of Hell, even in a whisper. . . . It was a voice that entered the whole body—was there, imploding, before the listener knew he had been filled with sound.
—Terry Kay, *The Year the Lights Came On*

The preacher with Bible in hand, standing behind the pulpit or pacing before the congregation, is the dominant image of the Protestant minister in Southern culture and its fiction. Whether Baptist or Methodist, Pentecostal or Presbyterian, the preacher is the one who stands and delivers within the congregation an authoritative interpretation of Scripture and life in the light of God. Christians in the South revere the sermon as *the* central location of the Divine speaking within Christian community. That so many people would sit through long, often rambling, disjointed sermons week after week attests to the power of the preached word within Southern culture. As Ralph Wood says about Flannery O'Connor's preachers, who emerge from the soil of Southern Protestantism, "Their preaching is not a quaint Southern habit; it is the Good News, the one Word whose awful demand engenders its saving response." Proclamation of the Word of God—preaching—has long been at the heart of the Protestant minister's self-understanding and congregational expectation. Indeed, Karl Barth referred to preaching as *the* distinctively Protestant sacrament.[1]

The understanding of the minister as preacher fully emerged in the South toward the end of the eighteenth century and was solidified by the middle of the nineteenth. Once it took hold, the designation "preacher" became fixed within Southern religious experience. The term "preacher" usually designates the ordained leader of the more conservative, evangelical, and rural or small-town expressions of Southern Christianity, but the term is also frequently used by mainline churches to designate the ordained leader. He, and to a lesser extent "she," is the visible representative of Protestant evangelical Christianity, Southern style. In proclaiming the word of God, the preacher aims to bring about for the hearers a personal experience of the saving grace of God or to provide instruction for faithful living.[2]

Fictional preachers appear in almost endless variety. Some are intoxicated with language and elevated by an emotional and spiritual fervor that they transmit to the congregation. Like the African American preacher, Rev. Alonzo Hickman, in Ralph Ellison's *Juneteenth*, they are "masters of ecstasy," who like great jazzmen can "allow for the transcendence of reality." Or like Lee Smith's independent Appalachian preacher, Virgil Shepherd, in *Saving Grace,* the preacher is charismatically gifted with a voice and delivery that draws the congregation into the sermon as a spoken event. "Even today, I don't know how to describe Daddy's voice, for that was surely one of his greatest blessings from the Lord. Daddy's voice made you feel good, like you were strong in the Lord, and proud to do his will." In content, rhetoric, and effect, preaching lies at the heart of Christian ministry in the South.[3]

But another side of preaching and preachers also comes out in Southern literature: the preacher as tiresome, meddling, moralistic, shallow, ignorant, bumbling, or irrelevant. When this happens, it's not just the minister who is being mocked, but the adverse qualities of preaching itself, the preacher's pulpit theatrics or mind-numbing mediocrity.

Boring, irrelevant, or both, many Southern preachers could put themselves to sleep in the pulpit. Southern fiction often contrasts the image of the preacher as amusing distraction with the preacher as colossal bore. One of the characters in Lisa Alther's *Original Sins* comments on an East Tennessee preacher: "The pastor droned on. . . . Mother and I endured the eternal sermon with downcast eyes. . . . Our pastor sure could talk, but to his credit, he didn't pound on hellfire and abuse. His topics were drier: church dogma."[4]

So many preachers populate Southern fiction that an entire book could be written on the subject. But here we will look briefly at three preachers who provide different angles of vision on the task and theology of preaching. Alonzo Hickman in Ralph Ellison's unfinished novel, *Juneteenth*, is a remarkable example of the African American Baptist preacher in the South. Rhetorical genius, emotional fervor, and congregational participation in the preaching event, hallmarks of African American preaching in the Baptist church of the South, are all evident in his preaching ministry. We see a preacher of a different denominational cast in Rev. Neil Eldridge, beloved pastor of Emery, Georgia, Methodist Church in Terry Kay's *The Year the Lights Came On*. And finally, we will look at the direct and testimonial preaching of the independent community church minister, Lee Avery, in Michael Morris's *A Place Called Wiregrass*. Through these fictional ministers we can see how preaching functions theologically and pastorally as God's word from above, a word among the people, and as a self-emptying word from below.

Giving Them Transcendence: The Word from Above in Ralph Ellison's *Juneteenth*

Ministers navigate a razor-thin theological edge when they preach. As Frederick Buechner says, "Anybody who preaches a sermon without realizing that he's heading straight for Scylla and Charybdis ought to try a safer more productive line of work, like laying eggs for instance." Audacious as it seems, the church claims that the sermon is the inspired word of God delivered by fallible human voices. "How are they to hear without someone to proclaim him?" Paul asks, for "faith comes from what is heard, and what is heard comes through the word of Christ" (Romans 10:14–17). The Reformers Calvin, Luther, and Zwingli all affirmed that preaching the word of God *is* the word of God. It's enough to give any preacher pause: God's word for the people rides in upon the frayed syntax of the preacher. Whether the minister likes it or not, and whether she feels the least bit competent or not, the preacher has accepted the task of conveying divine utterance.[5]

The congregation expects it, this word from above. And the minister knows the yearning. If any moment in the church's weekly rhythm promises transcendence, surely the preaching moment is it. If there is any place or time in which the preacher and the congregation can expect meeting with the Divine, surely it is in the temple when the one who is called to preach stands to deliver. Yet any preacher with even a smidgen of self-awareness knows that he is unworthy of the task. He stands before the expectant congregation, knowing he is just as human as they are, and dares to pluck words out of the air that are supposed to be charged with the mystery of God.

This task is at best a "burdensome joy." The minister may once in a while have "fire in his bones" that cannot be kept down, but he knows better than most, or should, that God cannot be summoned upon command: "The wind [Spirit] blows where it chooses" (John 3:8). The preacher may joyfully discover a ringing word from God during sermon preparation on Thursday only to hear it land with a dull thud when preaching it on Sunday. For this, John Chrysostom's advice seems timely: preachers need two basic attributes: "contempt of praise and force of eloquence."[6]

Still, congregations want and need transcendence—to have their hearts, minds, and imaginations renewed by the Spirit of God. The congregation seeks to be re-created in the image of Christ, to be raised with God's word above the enslavement of sin, beyond the idolatries of the age: self, consumerism, technological wizardry, nation, and class. More than anything else, it wants, sometimes with an unnamed longing, a terribly timid hope, to be born into the arms of the Easter-giving God. And it has every theological right to expect it if, as the church professes, preaching sets loose the word of God among the congregation.

The native Oklahoma novelist Ralph Ellison hears this longing for transcendence within the African American community and the Christian congregation. In *Juneteenth*, his complex novel of religion, race, and politics in the South, an uneducated but gifted Baptist preacher, Rev. Alonzo Hickman, preaches in various Southern states including Oklahoma, Texas, and Alabama during the Jim Crow era of the twentieth-century South, aiming to fill the congregation's yearning for transcendence. His sermons are rich with biblical allusion, African American colloquialisms, and the expert wordplay that characterize much of African American preaching in the South. We see this when Hickman explains to his protégé, Bliss, how he was summoned to preach on the occasion of Juneteenth, the traditional African American celebration of the proclamation of emancipation in Texas, on June 19, 1865:

> And the Master said, . . . "Hickman, Rise up on the Word and ride. All time is mine. . . . Just be prepared. Now get up there and ride!" And Bliss, I threw back my head and rode! It was like a riddle or a joke, but if so, it was the Lord's joke and I was playing it straight. And maybe that's what a preacher really is, he's the Lord's own straight man.

Hickman knows that he must ride the Word of God because this congregation depends upon his preaching to help deliver them from the Jim Crow vestiges of slavery. Their ongoing oppression at the hands of the white majority requires a religious response that provides transcendence. They can tolerate racism's degradation only if through worship they experience their liberated and true identity as sons and daughters of God. African American literary scholar Dolan Hubbard has observed, "The sustaining genius of unlettered and semiliterate black folk preachers is that they did not permit the people to die spiritually." So Hickman, the one whose voice can create "an atmosphere of bafflement and mystery," takes up the challenge of his calling. He understands that "a preacher is a man who carries God's load. And that's the whole earth, Bliss boy. The whole earth and all the people."[7]

Hickman knows the difference between congregational enthusiasm in worship and an authentic encounter with God. Yes, worship in the African American tradition is often joyful and emotionally cathartic, and the sermon provides a primary means of congregational celebration. But the ecstasy of spirited worship serves the purpose of meeting the Almighty God. As Barbara Holmes says in *Joy Unspeakable*, "The test of effective worship is not the fervor in the songs or the trance and dance; it is in the 'fruit' or evidence in the lives of those who enter into joy unspeakable." Hickman knows the difference and accepts the responsibility of helping the congregation, through preaching and worship, to ascend to the tabernacle of God.[8]

In all traditions, the language of preaching serves a much greater purpose than aesthetic pleasure. Hickman's jazzlike improvisation is much more than rhetorical skill and gifted oratory, though it certainly is that. He reminds all of us, especially the gifted orators among us, that at the heart of the calling resides the power of God's Word through words. He says to Bliss, his beloved son in the gospel, "Words are your business, boy. Not just *the* Word. Words are everything. The key to the Rock, the answer to the Question." Hickman honors words themselves because through them God chooses to create ("Then God *said,* 'Let there be light'" [Genesis 1:3]). Godly words impart life itself.[9]

With his inspired words, the preacher creates a sensory, intellectual, and spiritual experience for the congregation that will lift them high enough that God may be apprehended and true moral order restored. Trusting the words she speaks, the preacher becomes a servant to them. All her rhetorical brilliance—from use of imagery, intonation, allusion, humor, pathos, and delivery—serves the greater purpose of joining the congregation's hands with the hands of a just God.

The preacher is not a resident word magician. She cannot wave the magic voice wand on any given Sunday and bring down God from the mountain. The otherness of God will not be bottled and delivered for satisfying consumption at eleven o'clock once a week, despite efforts today to make worship "user friendly." God will be God. As God reminds the inquiring Moses, "I AM WHO I AM" (Exodus 3:14). When the lightning of God strikes—the word from above—it usually smokes the preacher first. On behalf of the congregation, the preacher listens attentively for the word of God within Scripture and within the life of the congregation and the world. And when the word of God arrives, he climbs "up there where the fire is so hot it's ice, and ice so cold it burns like fire."[10]

Too Good a Community to Be Tore Apart by Arguin':
The Word Among Community
in Terry Kay's *The Year the Lights Came On*

Georgia novelist Terry Kay shines the spotlight from another angle on preaching. In *The Year the Lights Came On*, it's 1947 and the Rev. Neil Eldridge is the retiring pastor of Emery Methodist Church located outside Royston, Georgia. Eldridge is a beloved pastor and a "majestic old man," whose pastoral preaching has shaped the local community and congregation.

Eldridge, like Ellison's Rev. Hickman, possesses a distinctive voice, one that conveys spiritual power. His unstudied but eloquent preaching, creation-like, draws people out of darkness into the light of God:

> He had not studied great theologies in a seminary, and God, or the Bishop, had never called him to a great church. But his voice had numbed even the most scholarly and decorated churchmen, and he was often summoned to Atlanta to deliver prayers of especial meaning. His was a voice able to penetrate the latched, inner iron gate of Hell, even in a whisper; a voice able to coax sinners writhing in damnation up from Fire and Brimstone, up through the narrow slit of brilliant light that was heaven. It was a voice that entered the *whole* body—was there, imploding, before the listener knew he had been filled with sound.

But it is not the *quality* of Eldridge's voice that is the issue, not a particular tonal quality that makes him successful. The mistaken belief that there is such a mysterious quality that ensures success leads some preachers to adopt phony pulpit voices, which usually only grate on or

amuse their listeners. Rather, Kay's description—"a voice able to penetrate the latched, inner iron gate of Hell, even in a whisper"—lets us
imagine the effect of the voice. What is important is how God through
the voice affects the listeners, not that only a certain kind of voice can
have such effect. What rings true for the hearers is that the preacher's
voice—smooth or rough, slow as molasses or jerky as a tilt-a-whirl—has
been claimed by God. When that happens, as with Rev. Eldridge, people are no longer listening to the preacher's voice but for the word of
God within the words and voice of the preacher.[11]

The authority of Eldridge's preaching comes from his standing in the
congregation and community. He is their pastor, and his sermons get a
hearing because he is committed to the Methodist congregation as their
shepherd. Though an itinerant Methodist pastor, accustomed to move
according to the "three-year pulse beat of God's call to carton-and-box
belongings and move to another white, clapboard church in another
white, clapboard setting of farm families," Eldridge is the elder pastor
who offers a lifetime of pastoral understanding and wise preaching to
the congregation. He preaches into the everyday world of the community. With them, he hangs on to God when trouble threatens; he leads
them in praise when joy breaks through.[12]

Eldridge's main theme in preaching is the "vulnerability of Jesus." After
a lifetime of Sunday sermons and the slow decline of memory brought on
by age, Eldridge remains "quite certain of Jesus' vulnerability."

> The assailable Jesus—was the catalyst of God's greatness; else how
> would the triumphant Jesus—the invulnerable God-man be clearly
> understood by congregations who knew more of injury than of con-
> quering. Once in a sermon, he had even spoken in an admirable way
> of the crucifix of the Catholic church. He had his own philosophy of
> that venerable symbol: it was God's screech of pain, . . . a scene to be
> studied and remembered, and a scene made worthy by the assurance
> of the Empty Cross—". . . *our* symbol," he proudly proclaimed.

Eldridge's theological grounding in the incarnation of God through
Jesus Christ orients him pastorally to the wounds of the Emery community. He preaches out of the suffering of God in order finally to bring
the congregation to the assurance of Easter, the empty cross. His theology runs close to the ground where the people live. Walking beside
them, Eldridge can gently steer the congregation toward the hope of the
resurrection.[13]

The formative power of Eldridge's preaching becomes evident during an occasion of congregational conflict. The community is divided over the guilt or innocence of Freeman, a local teenager, who has been accused of stealing from his employer and is now on the run, hiding out in the swamp. Class divisions in the community deepen as the poor, working-class laborers support Freeman's innocence while the owners and management decry his guilt. The rancor is serious:

> Because it was Freeman, and Freeman was of the Other Class ("Not like everyone else" was the phrase), the accusation became a drama of class distinction. It was an argument of ugliness and anyone with grit willingly took sides. . . . Yet, in the frenzy of Freeman's supposed crime—the serious debate of serious men and women in serious disagreement—a curious effect developed: Freeman, the person, was ignored; Freeman, the symbol, became a competition of words said and words not heard.

As with many conflicts in small Southern communities, this one spills over into the local church, where it festers beneath the veneer of religious respectability and becomes all the more infected because no one addresses it.[14]

Rev. Eldridge does not shrink from the human conflict playing out within the church. He can look out from the pulpit and see the quarrelers—those who support Freeman's innocence on the right and those who believe in his guilt on the left. As a mature pastor, he has probably been in the middle of similar congregational conflicts. Eldridge does not ignore the strife; he does not try to pour oil upon the water. He does not call in a conflict management consultant. Rather, he assumes his place and his responsibility as preacher and pastor of a hurting congregation, and he does the thing that God and the church have called him to do: preach the gospel.

His sermon uses Scripture and analogy to help the congregation see their current conflict in the light of God's word and reminds them of their ethical responsibility for each other.

> He did not speak of Freeman, not by name. He selected the story of Cain and Abel as his sermon topic, and he preached with such remembered vitality he seemed wholly different. . . . He spoke a parable of brothers and forgiveness, and he challenged each member to read and remember the church motto hanging over the piano: I am only one, I cannot do everything, but I can do something. And what I can do, by the grace of God, I ought to do.

Then, true to Southern evangelical religious form, preacher Eldridge

> closed the service with the first and last verses of "Just as I Am," and
> a benediction that left every man, woman, and child limp with
> unworthiness. It was a benediction inscribed on the flint of our souls,
> a masterful solicitation of God's wonderfulness and His power to
> heal the wounds of strife.

With this sermon and worship service, the preacher has fulfilled his bidding to speak the Word of God within Christian community. He must now wait upon the Spirit of God to work within the congregation as the Spirit wills.[15]

In this case (and I grant Terry Kay fictional license), the Spirit works quickly to bring about congregational reconciliation. Reminded by the sermon of who they are as rebellious yet loving sons and daughters of God, the members move toward one another in forgiveness. "Outside, after services, there were mumbled, awkward apologies for misbehavior." In an uncharacteristically open exchange for rural Southerners whose conversation is usually oblique rather than direct, the members seek and extend forgiveness. Even their normal ways of communicating have been transformed by the sermon:

> "Preacher's right. Fightin' among ourselves is wrong, bad wrong."
> "What I said last week, well I didn't mean nothin'. Y'all know I
> didn't mean nothin', I hope."
> "My fault as much as yours . . ."
> "I reckon I started it. . . ."
> "This is too good a community to be tore apart by arguin'."
> "Yeah . . ."

With these open yet simple declarations of confession and forgiveness, the church members have come home to themselves. It is no coincidence that following the worship service the Sunday school lesson is on the Prodigal Son. The church members now speak their true language of grace and pardon. They affirm the riches of Christian community. Through a sermon preached into the hard cracks of community life, they have been named by Scripture, found, and received by God.[16]

Rev. Eldridge, who appears only in this one brief scene, is a mainline Protestant, Southern clergyman who knows that preaching is to "equip the saints . . . for ministry" (Ephesians 4:11–13). In this case, the sermon equips the saints for the practice of confession and forgiveness.

Rev. Hickman in *Juneteenth* shows how preaching discloses the transcendent word of God. Here we see how it also forms and transforms the behavior and habits of the congregation so that, over time, the Christian congregation becomes shaped in the likeness of Christ. Without the sermon and the trustworthy humanity of Rev. Eldridge, community reconciliation would not have been possible. In other words, preaching and the Scripture it is based upon are ethically demanding. In Rev. Neil Eldridge, we see a minister who shows how preaching the word of God within community truly edifies.[17]

Lower than a Snake's Belly: The Word Below in Michael Morris's *A Place Called Wiregrass*

In Michael Morris's novel *A Place Called Wiregrass*, Lee Avery is pastor of the independent Wiregrass Community Church, located in southeastern Alabama. Avery is Caucasian, thirty years old, a former drug abuser and criminal, who has become the ordained leader of a blue-collar, nondenominational congregation.

Congregations like his reflect the widespread phenomenon of the independent community church in the South. These community congregations, conservative evangelical in theology and congregational in polity, have sprung up across the South in the past fifty years, partly in response to the decline of mainline Protestant churches and partly because in the South evangelical Christianity seems to always find a way to proliferate. If the mainline denominations will not host it (Southern Baptists excepted), Southern conservative evangelical piety will find another house where its members can seek individual salvation from the torments of sin, read the Bible as a literal moral guide, and give heartfelt expression to their emotions in worship.

Avery's preaching cannot be understood apart from his drug abuse and criminal past. His preaching is a response to a dramatic personal experience of salvation. He came into Christian ministry through a jail-cell conversion brought about by the prayers and tears of his grandmamma, in a clear parallel with the familiar story of St. Augustine's conversion through the tears of his mother, Monica. As Avery testifies in a sermon,

> I've done it all, lived it all, and lost it all. I've been so low that I stole money from my grandma's social security check to buy crack. But,

praise God, when I was sitting in jail after robbing a liquor store on a winter night, my grandma didn't give up on me. She came to visit me. . . . She begged me to lean on Jesus. . . . She said that she had prayed for me to reach rock bottom. . . . And then she told me why. Because when you're lower than a snake's belly and you're lying there looking at the mud, all the sudden you can look up and realize that the Lord is Everything. "Surgery on sin's cataracts," she called it.

This one converting moment, recounted in down-home Southern speak, is what orders Lee Avery's understanding of Christian faith and his own approach to ministry and preaching. True to the bedrock belief of Southern evangelical piety, nothing else matters unless we know and believe that Jesus "wants us to rest on Him, to lean on Him. And friends, Jesus will carry our burdens."[18]

Avery's preaching is testimonial, a favored approach to the sermon in the South. For Avery and many like him, personal religious experience is the primary authority for Christian faith and action. He appeals to his own faith struggles and conversion in order to initiate or build upon similar religious experiences of his hearers. "And don't sit there thinking who else needs to hear this message," Lee said, suddenly standing. "We're all the same in God's sight. We all have to take the same step regardless of our circumstance." Aware of the corruption of sin in his own life, Avery pleads with his hearers in the words of the simple Christian song: "Turn Your Eyes upon Jesus."[19]

Before we dismiss Avery's preaching and theology as Southern "primitive," we need to take a closer look. His faith appears individualistic, and his view of baptism is nonsacramental: "Baptism is just a public declaration. The heart is where it really counts." There is little evidence of careful reasoning or historically informed approaches to ministry in his work, but he crackles with gospel fire, in contrast to the status-quo ministry of the Methodist minister, Rev. Winters. When Winters fails to stand up to his congregation in the face of its objections to a shelter for battered women, a project proposed by Miss Claudia, a wealthy dowager, she says of him, "Bless his heart, the man's got a backbone of a jellyfish." She chastises him: "Get down on your knees and pray for the church. Too many of them are playing church rather than worshipping the Lord." A maintainer of the status quo, Winters fears genuine religious experience. "Others are very comfortable with our worship service," he explains. To use a phrase of Will Willimon, Winters has "blacked out," forgotten who he is as a servant of Christ. He is a func-

tionary of the church but not a pastor or preacher enlivened by the resurrection power of Jesus Christ.[20]

In contrast, Avery's sermons and actions sizzle along the rails of conviction that God is doing a new thing in Jesus Christ. He sides with the
poor and abused of the community by supporting the development of
the shelter. When the proposal is temporarily defeated by the community guardians of the status quo, he preaches to his discouraged congregation that "when you go through bad stuff and don't have answers, you
got to focus on Christ . . . Christ, not circumstance. We can either let
the circumstances control us, or we can ask the Lord to carry it for us."
These are the hopeful words of a preacher who recognizes that, as John
Calvin suggested, putting on the lens of Scripture allows Christians to
see the world in a new light. Avery points the congregation's vision
toward the real world of the kingdom of God, where the hungry are fed,
the poor are blessed, and the suffering receive God, rather than the supposed world of daily circumstance.[21]

The fact is that Lee Avery's preaching connects with the members of
his congregation because he understands experientially just how far God
will stoop—"lower than a snake's belly"—to raise the fallen, and he uses
their own language to tell them. He announces a gospel of a Savior who
enters into human struggle not with strength but with weakness. To his
hardworking, hard-living, blue-collar congregation he proclaims a
Christ who eats with sinners.[22]

Lee Avery isn't seminary trained, and his manners are not those of
the well-polished sanctuary. But in a world where family violence, drug
addiction, unemployment, and teenage pregnancy are not statistics in a
newspaper but hard, cold facts of daily existence, the preacher had better know a Jesus who has dirt on his hands and blood on his shirt if he
hopes to announce good news. If the word of God has any chance of
entering into the lives of these people, it will enter not in the Johannine
fashion from above but in the Lukan fashion from below. Lee Avery is
not much interested in God upon the throne, but he puts great stock in
the Jesus who though he was in the form of God took the "form of a
slave, being born in human likeness, . . . and became obedient to the
point of death—even death on a cross" (Philippians 2:6–8). The
preacher's word of God from below finds a home among these hardworking, hard-living Southern believers. Through his testimonial
preaching, the minister points the congregation toward the "Jesus who
died for us [and] gives us a second chance," a Jesus who performs
"surgery on sin's cataracts."[23]

I'm Here to Encourage You to Go A-Preaching

In Robert Olen Butler's short story "Up by Heart," set on the outskirts of Sparta, Tennessee, God speaks to Hurshel Hudgens, who has memorized the entire Bible "up by heart." God calls him in Southern dialect, "I'm here to encourage you to go a-preaching," and then tells Hudgens, whose knees are going wobbly, "In the beginning was the word. I've always been a talker."[24]

Preachers take their cue from a loquacious God, revealed in Scripture and understood in church tradition as a creating and redeeming Word. Preachers offer their words to this talkative God, trusting that in God's own way the word "shall not return . . . empty" (Isaiah 55:11). In the storytelling South, where the Bible is still in some families and churches gotten "up by heart"—though sadly less so today than in previous generations—believers cling to the power of words and stories to disclose the mystery of God. The writer Doris Betts acknowledges this in talking about her own Bible-steeped upbringing in the Associate Reformed Presbyterian Church:

> But what I did absorb was the conviction that the Image of God was actually linguistic, that what we called "soul" could only be made manifest in language seen, said, heard, read, riddled and rhymed, parsed, even scribbled by children, on notebooks, in lemon juice, without any tangible loss of magic. Words were the power inside us. Words also had the power to materialize a hand out of thin air to write the future. . . . Words could pull cripples to their feet.

Preachers who haven't at least an inkling of appreciation for the Word in words probably have no business stepping into the pulpit. The church will be deformed, and the preacher will be wasting everyone's time including her own. The preacher is a word peddler, and the church where she preaches, in Martin Luther's evocative phrase, is a "speech house." While listening to sermons, we must take our eyes and stick them in our ears.[25]

Southern stories yield a variety of fictional preachers. Some, like Ralph Ellison's Alonzo Hickman, preach with such imaginative power and rhetorical genius that they draw us into the reaches of heaven, where we all bow down before the throne and cry, "Glory." Other preachers, like Terry Kay's Rev. Neil Eldridge or Michael Morris's Lee Avery, proclaim the incarnate Word of God that runs close to the ground, where it transforms individuals and congregations into the new creation of

Jesus Christ. Either way, once the Christian believer hears and accepts God's call to "go a-preaching," words and voice become servant to the word and voice of God, who speaks and worlds come to be, who whispers a name—"Mary"—and eyes are opened.

If fiction in some sense mirrors reality, the sheer number of preachers who appear in contemporary Southern fiction give some credence to William Willimon's observation that he sees a return to the minister *as preacher* as a guiding metaphor of ministry today. In the hands of the preachers we have met in this chapter, the Word of God is secure; the calling to preach is trustworthy.[26]

But in Southern literature as in real life, many ministers do not fare as well. Some, like the evangelists to whom we will now turn, pitch their revival tents under clouds of suspicion; they conduct their baptisms in streams of sarcasm. As in Flannery O'Connor's short story "The River," the skeptical Mr. Paradise says about the evangelist and healer Rev. Bevel Summers, "Pass the hat and give this kid his money. That's what he's here for."[27]

3

You Didn't Even Count Before

The Minister as Evangelist

"If I baptize you," the preacher said, "you'll be able to go to the Kingdom of Christ. You'll be washed in the river of suffering son, and you'll
go by the deep river of life. Do you want that? . . . You won't be the same
again," the preacher said. "You'll count."
    —Rev. Bevel Summers, in Flannery O'Connor's "The River"

IF YOU ARE HERE YOU ARE IN TROUBLE
MANY HAVE DIED HERE, LOST FROM BOTH MOTHER
AND CHRIST OUR LORD JESUS.
THIS IS HELL, FRIEND.
LET ME TAKE YOU TOWARD A HAPPY WORLD
The Bryon Egan Ministries
In front of you as you stand.
    —Barry Hannah, *Yonder Stands Your Orphan*

Of all the colorful characters crowding the pews and pulpits of Southern religion and fiction, none is more flamboyant than the evangelist.
Jumpy and eager to testify, with his singular intent to stir up gospel conviction, the evangelist pants and paces and promises sweet salvation
from the sin of the world.

Many people have fun at the expense of the evangelist; he's an easy
target for ridicule. With one eye upon the collection plate and another
upon the bodily enticements of the congregants, his hypocrisy, especially his weakness regarding the "sins of the flesh," is an easy target. But
as we will see, not all evangelists can be so easily dismissed. As always,
the devout evangelist plays a crucial role in Christian ministry. His
speech announces the good news (the *euangelion*, the gospel) of God's
salvation through Jesus Christ and urges hearers to "repent and believe
in the gospel." Far from being religious snake-oil salesmen, some evangelists live with the awful burden that God has chosen them to unmask
and redeem human evil and suffering. Their words and hands bring
good news; they evangelize and save (Mark 1:15).[1]

The true evangelists are dead serious about their calling. They believe
that every day Christ is seeking the broken, the wounded, the least, and
the lost to invite into a new order—the kingdom of God. Even if Southern evangelists understand the new order in highly individualistic terms,

they believe that conversion from the old and sinful self to the new and saved self is what matters. At its best, there is a theological urgency and intent to the ministry of the evangelist. God calls the evangelist to make Christ known to others even if they do not want to hear. As Flannery O'Connor said about the religious urgency of her characters, "To the hard of hearing you shout, and for the almost-blind you draw large and startling figures." So we now turn to one of O'Connor's Southern evangelists to deepen our understanding of this office of the ministry.[2]

You Didn't Even Count Before: Baptizing Your Pain in the River of Life in Flannery O'Connor's "The River"

Entering the fictional world of Flannery O'Connor may be the closest that a reader can come to baptism without actually being dunked; in many cases, it is much more efficacious. The Southern settings are familiar enough: small towns, countryside, and the anonymous cities that encroach upon them. But her oddball characters with names like Mason Tarwater (*The Violent Bear It Away*), Hulga Hopewell ("Good Country People"), and O. E. Parker ("Parker's Back") move across the Southern landscape, making such blunt declarations and startling discoveries that those who encounter them either run like hell away from them or gaze, rapt, as they speak and enact their convicting truth upon the hearer. When, for example, the fundamentalist prophet Mason Tarwater gets in the face of his great-nephew and warns, "Even the mercy of the Lord burns," many will start looking for an exit. But if they manage to stay put, by story's end, when the nephew has taken up his great-uncle's calling—"GO WARN THE CHILDREN OF GOD OF THE TERRIBLE SPEED OF MERCY"—the hearers themselves may well be looking for the regenerating waters of baptism.

In O'Connor's Christ-haunted world, evangelists like Bevel Summers in "The River" often take center stage. The Rev. Bevel Summers preaches and heals at "the river" outside of an unnamed Southern city. One of his faithful supporters is Mrs. Connin, working poor, the no-nonsense caretaker of five-year-old Harry Ashfield. Harry's parents, nonreligious, self-absorbed, and urbane, have no emotional attachment to their own son and provide him with no spiritual training. When Mrs. Connin carries Harry to the river to meet the evangelist, he does not understand what is going on. Harry knows nothing of baptism, faith healing, or evangelical preaching. Religiously, Harry is a blank slate, but emotionally and spiritually, he is deeply scarred by parental neglect. "He seemed mute and patient, like an old sheep waiting to be let out." Under the tutelage of the well-meaning and religiously devout Mrs. Connin, Harry is ripe for a spiritual awakening, which Rev. Bevel Summers knows how to provide.[3]

Summers is a John the Baptist of the Deep South. When we first see him, he stands knee-deep in the river, singing.

> His face was all bone and red light reflected from the river. He looked as if he might have been nineteen years old. He was singing in a high twangy voice, above the singing on the bank, and he kept his hands behind him and his head tilted back.

When the singing stops, Summers stands silent for a minute, then he cuts loose with his call to salvation. He exhorts the hearers that his purpose is spiritual salvation, not physical healing. "If you ain't come for Jesus, you ain't come for me. If you just come to see can you leave your pain in the river, you ain't come for Jesus. You can't leave your pain in the river. I never told nobody that." Though word has traveled throughout the region that Bevel Summers is a miracle worker, as a true evangelist he will not let miracles become the focus of his ministry. To the woman who says that she has seen him cure people, he retorts, "You might as well go home if that's what you come for."[4]

It turns out that this backwoods, primitive evangelist is a rustic theological sophisticate. While Summers may not know the biblical etymology of "salvation"—*sōzō*—"to be healed or saved"—he knows the potential problems that can occur when desperate people seek healing and salvation. He will not allow the physical needs of the crowd to obscure the more fundamental need for wholeness in Christ. Like Jesus' healing in the Gospels, he wants to point beyond the healing to the greater glory of God. Rather than support the dualism of his followers who separate the physical from the spiritual, he plunges them into the fullness of the sacrificial love of Christ.

> Listen to what I got to say, you people! There ain't but one river and that's the River of Life, made out of Jesus' Blood. That's the river you have to lay your pain in, in the River of Faith, in the River of Life, in the River of love, in the rich red river of Jesus' Blood, you people!

In Summers's baptismal invitation, evangelical fundamentalism meets orthodox Catholicism. Though typically Protestant in his call to con-

version, Summer's stress upon baptism as removing original sin is deeply
Catholic:

> All the rivers come from that one River and go back to it like it was
> the ocean sea and if you believe, you can lay your pain in that River
> and get rid of it because that's the River that was made to carry sin.
> It's a River full of pain itself, pain itself, moving toward the Kingdom
> of Christ, to be washed away, slow, you people, slow as this here old
> red water river round my feet.[5]

Young Harry Ashfield, it turns out, wants what the evangelist is offering. Or more accurately, Harry wants what *he* understands Summers to
be offering. When Mrs. Connin presents Harry for baptism ("Swang
him over here," Summers says), Harry first thinks it is a joke, because
"where he lived everything was a joke." But he quickly perceives that
"nothing the preacher said or did was a joke." Evangelist Summers is
playing for keeps. When Harry tells Summers he doesn't know about
baptism, the evangelist launches into a rudimentary catechism. "If I
Baptize you, you'll be able to go to the Kingdom of Christ. You'll be
washed in the river of suffering, son, and you'll go by the deep river of
life. . . . You won't be the same again. You'll count." Nothing could be
more inviting to the neglected Harry than the promise of "counting,"
of truly mattering to someone else, for ignored by his parents, the child
is quietly desperate for the sustaining love of a true home. When Summers asks, "Do you want that?" Harry's answer comes without hesita-
tion: "Yes." With that exchange between the lonely child and the earnest
evangelist, the stage is set for Harry's full embrace of the watery world
of Christian baptism, an embrace that Harry understands in the concrete and literal way of a five-year-old: "I won't go back to the apartment
then. I'll go under the river."

> "All right, I'm going to Baptize you now," and without more warn-
> ing, he tightened his hold and swung him upside down and plunged
> his head into the water. He held him under while he said the words
> of Baptism and then he jerked him up again and looked sternly at
> the gasping child. Bevel's eyes were dark and dilated. "You count
> now," the preacher said. "You didn't even count before."[6]

The evangelist's words and baptismal action provide Harry with a
brand-new understanding of where he belongs and what matters. He
has passed over (converted) from an old self to a new self through

immersion in Christ. Later, when Harry returns to his parents, he tries to explain to his mother what has happened. When she angrily asks him, "What did that dolt of a preacher say?" Harry signals the full force of his immersion. "He said I'm not the same now. I count." Predictably, the vain mother misses this cue from her redeemed child and moves away from him, "swaying her hips lightly."[7]

From here on, the five-year-old Harry literally follows the call of the River of Life. The evangelist has made the river and its healing so inviting that in the mind of a five-year-old, the logical thing to do is to return for good to the River. Harry leaves the apartment without even being missed by his parents. He retraces the route to the river and eagerly bounds into the water to embrace its life.

> He intended not to fool with preachers any more but to Baptize himself and to keep on going this time until he found the Kingdom of Christ in the river. He didn't mean to waste any more time. He put his head under the water at once and pushed forward.

Initially puzzled and then angered that the river seems to push him back up to the surface, Harry thinks that it has all been a joke. "He thought how far he had come for nothing and he began to splash and kick the filthy river." Then in desperation and frightened by the appearance of a man who attempts to stop him, Harry plunges under the water again.

> He plunged under once and this time, the waiting current caught him like a long gentle hand and pulled him swiftly forward and down. For an instant he was overcome with surprise; then since he was moving quickly and knew that he was getting somewhere, all his fury and fear left him.[8]

O'Connor clearly intends to shock us with the baptismal death and life of Harry. On the literal level, his is a tragedy born of misunderstanding and parental neglect. But on the sacramental level, Harry has entered into the waters of life that unite him with Christ. Commenting on this story, O'Connor said,

> I am very aware that for a majority of my readers, baptism is a meaningless rite, and so in my novel I have to see that this baptism carries enough awe and mystery to jar the reader into some kind of emotional recognition of its significance. . . . Distortion in this case is an instrument; exaggeration has a purpose, and the whole structure of

the story or novel has been made what it is because of belief. This is not the kind of distortion that destroys; it is the kind that reveals, or should reveal.

Through baptism, Harry knows who he is—a child of God—and where he belongs—in the kingdom of Christ. He even has a new name, calling himself "Bevel" just like the preacher. Through the preaching and invitation of the evangelist Summers, Harry-Bevel embraces the fullness of the apostle Paul's baptismal creed: "buried with him by baptism into death, . . . [we are] raised from the dead through the glory of the Father" (Romans 6:4).[9]

As I noted earlier, Southern writers and church critics are often quick to lampoon the country evangelist. He is an easy target for both satirists and the outraged, who want to expose religious chicanery. But some of these writers and critics are the very "cultured despisers" of religion that Flannery O'Connor wants to disarm with a character such as Rev. Bevel Summers. Like John the Baptist, Bevel Summers traipses across the South Georgia countryside with only one message worth telling: "Repent, for the kingdom of heaven has come near" (Matthew 3:2). O'Connor sees Summers as a straight messenger of an offensive truth: "If you ain't come for Jesus, you ain't come for me." If we take the Southern evangelist's message to heart, as O'Connor intends, then we encounter a God worth living and dying for. If we humor him and his message, O'Connor seems to say, the joke is on us.

Hard-edged evangelism like Bevel's has fallen into disfavor in the South and everywhere else as well. Christianity has grown cozy with culture. The blunt message of the rough-hewn evangelist has been replaced by soothing invitations to "seeker-friendly" worship. We promise comfort and familiar music to the nonbeliever rather than life-altering decisions to follow a crucified and resurrected Savior. Church membership is substituted for gospel conviction, and Christian witness amounts to showing up for worship at eleven o'clock on Sunday mornings.

Just what is Christian evangelism in early-twenty-first-century North America anyway? O'Connor's river-wading Bevel Summers leaves us with the suspicion that we may have forgotten what it means to call persons to commitment to Jesus Christ because most of us belong to congregations and denominations where so little is required and nothing is really at stake. Our evangelical appeals sound more like soft sells of a cozy lifestyle (me and my friend Jesus) than startling summons to drown ourselves in the waters of new life. We know that the shenanigans of the tent revivalist and the slick sells of the televangelist ring false, but where is the genuine encounter with Christ and his followers that summons us to lose ourselves for the sake of the gospel?

Behold, the Zombie of the Empty:
Preaching for the Lost and Dead of All Causes
in Barry Hannah's *Yonder Stands Your Orphan*

The edgy Rev. Byron Egan of Barry Hannah's *Yonder Stands Your Orphan* is an evangelist of striking originality, who might point us in the right direction. Reverend Egan shatters the mold of the Southern Protestant evangelist. One of the many eccentrics who zigzag through this rambunctious novel, Rev. Byron Egan is "a reformed biker, gambler, and drug addict, still with a ponytail, brown-gray, and a large black Maltese cross tattooed on his right cheek." A convert to nondenominational Protestantism, he is a "man immoderate in both callings, dissolute and sacred." Egan resides in the fictional Eagle Lake community of the Mississippi Delta, somewhere north of Vicksburg, where he is the self-appointed minister of the independent and rural "Church of the Open Doors."[10]

A reformed criminal, Egan pulls no punches in his evangelical bout with moral corruption. He confronts pimps and prostitutes, stoned musicians and car thieves, child abusers and killers. But he reserves his most righteous indignation for the casinos of Vicksburg, and he preaches with laser-like intensity against the social havoc caused by legalized gambling.

> He was preaching against the casino now, this nearby hell, a factory of thievery. . . . He preached about hollow and slick men and slot machine hags with no souls. The leering zombies schooled to rob the poor and sad in the name of fun. Worse than liquor were the glamour and baying of Mammonites, who turned the soul into nothing but the arithmetic of want.

In one sermon, Egan takes the Southern evangelist's penchant for pulpit drama to a new level. He ties off his arm with a necktie and plunges a hypodermic needle filled with holy water into a bulging vein. Drawing out pale blood and showing it to the congregation, he preaches, "This is what God gave us, not the green, gray dirty thing we call cash.

Filthy lucre. Filthy, how the old scribe knew it." Egan is not your run-of-the-mill tent revivalist of the South. He reserves almost as much scorn for the moral hypocrisy and money-worshiping false evangelists—the likes of Jim and Tammy Bakker or Jimmy Swaggart—as he does for the casino operators of Southern Mississippi.[11]

Egan the evangelist backs up his words with action. He marches straight into the maw of the gambling monster and seeks to rescue converts from the belly of the beast. He paces through the casinos, passing out his business cards.

> IF YOU ARE HERE YOU ARE IN TROUBLE
> MANY HAVE DIED HERE, LOST FROM BOTH MOTHER
> AND CHRIST OUR LORD JESUS.
> THIS IS HELL, FRIEND.
> LET ME TAKE YOU TOWARD A HAPPY WORLD.
> The Bryon Egan Ministries
> In front of you as you stand.

On one such evangelical expedition, he encounters Man Mortimer, a one-man vice operation with big hair, "a liaison for stolen cars and a runner of whores," whom the law can't touch and whom "religion had neither formed nor harmed." Man Mortimer's capacity for evil is limitless, matched only by Egan's zeal to redeem him from sin's destruction. When they meet, Egan says, "You're wicked all the way through. Another day I'd already have jacked up a switchblade to your throat and you'd be forgetting you look like Conway Twitty." Knowing the depth of evil that he confronts in Man Mortimer, the evangelist Egan is relentless. As he says to himself, "When he worked with evil, he worked with evil."[12]

No one is safe from Rev. Egan's socially attuned sermons. He is an evangelist of the Deep South who knows firsthand the very sin that he so acidly rails against. He is fearless in his evangelical crusade to pronounce the redemptive love of Jesus among the orphaned, the victimized, and the violent offenders of Eagle Lake.

Byron Egan is a different kind of evangelist than appears in a great deal of Southern fiction. His raw preaching echoes the evangelists of Flannery O'Connor, who relentlessly pursue individual salvation, but his social gospel expands the boundaries of evangelism. In his opposition to gambling, prostitution, child abuse, and a host of other social ills, Egan shares kinship with the abolitionists and temperance crusaders of the nineteenth and early twentieth centuries. His inventive and confrontational preaching weds social action and evangelism into a new marriage. Egan wages spiritual warfare against the powers and principalities of social evil personified in Man Mortimer. He is not simply seeking the redemption of the individual from personal vice. Rather, Egan wants to lay an ax to the root of evil. In one pointed sermon, he preaches directly to Man Mortimer.

> Are you, sir, Elvis, Wayne Newton, Sinatra or the wolvine Michael Jackson, child eater? Those Las Vegas—greased and damned? Or are you only some shadow Lounge Punk, wanting to be big in lights? I know you, friend. I have been kin to you. . . . Mr. Wannabe Caesar's Palace Puppy, oh you're sick all right. . . . Is your hair some kind of Goddamned Event?

Egan cranks up the voltage of the sermon because he is not "contending against flesh and blood, but against the principalities, against the powers, against the world rulers of this present darkness" (Ephesians 6:12 RSV). Who would stand for such a focused homiletic harangue other than a callous offender gripped by evil?[13]

Yet, Egan is not without concern for Mortimer's lost humanity. In the evangelist's eyes, Mortimer is an *orphan*, a wayfaring stranger like everyone else in the novel, who needs the mercy of Christ. As Mortimer slides into self-destruction, Egan sees his vulnerability and extends understanding to him if not compassion. "What we have is one old sinner out there trying to be legion. . . . He is nearing his breakdown." Though Mortimer wastes away in the novel, rotting from the inside out, and winds up babbling in Parchman Prison, Egan's vision of God's kingdom seems to be merciful enough to include him.[14]

Egan has been too far down the road of destruction himself to turn others away from the house of redemption, however dim their vision might be. He preaches at the Church of Open Doors, "open for the lost and dead of all causes." He reminds his flock that "the definition of a church is open, isn't it?" And into the independent, rural Mississippi country church, he gathers a whole host of local eccentrics and orphans who long for home. As Barry Hannah comments, echoing the theology of his own character, "We have all worked in the foyer of the lunatic asylum. Release and deliverance *by* work is all we know. But we pray and beg for something else across the river and into the shade of the trees. For me, that is where Christ stands."[15]

The members of Egan's flock are sad and desperate yet hopeful and tender as he points them toward their salvation. Egan communicates the radical openness of the kingdom of God, preaching, for example, at a funeral service for a community member who has committed suicide:

[There is] so much cloudiness here as to shut up the meaner of us who wanted to keep souls out of heaven. Heaven has many houses, very big and wide. Many mansions, many houses, as the Savior promised us, or He would not have told us so in His words. Many and large.

In the backwaters of Eagle Lake, Mississippi, Evangelist Byron Egan announces the good news among the down and out clearly enough to gather under one roof a community of misshapen believers who, with nowhere else to turn but toward grace, resemble the original New Testament followers of Christ: the widows and orphans, the blind and the lame, the despised and rejected. "Once you were not a people, but now you are God's people; once you had not received mercy, but now you have received mercy," says the New Testament writer of 1 Peter (2:10). The people of Egan's Church of the Open Door are like those rough-hewn New Testament living stones being built up into God's house, upon Christ the cornerstone.[16]

The being-saved riffraff of Byron Egan's Church of the Open Door are the ones whom the established mainline Protestant churches of the South often fail to see, much less know how to reach with the gospel. Many of us mainline ministers and congregations are so comfortable with North America's culture of ease and acquisition that we rarely imagine how we might make contact with those who live on the margins of middle-class respectability.

Byron Egan's provocative evangelism challenges ministers in the contemporary church. His emboldened approach to call others out from their personal and social diseases—from gambling to alcohol, pornography to violence—challenges the contemporary church's moral timidity within a culture that is awash in destructive behavior, including the rampant materialism headlined on gaudy casino marquees. One of our biggest sins is our own middle-class complacency in the face of numerous other social diseases such as grinding poverty, lack of adequate health care for all the nation's residents, a minimum wage that cannot sustain the working poor, and international warfare that saps the nation's resources and rains havoc upon other cultures. Yet the pulpit is mostly silent about these sins, as if the good news of the gospel means nothing at all with respect to these gaping sins. Surely evangelism is concerned about the well-being of all of society and not just about our own personal comfort and individual salvation. Byron Egan's unapologetic sharing of the gospel with anyone who will hear reminds the church that our primary mission is to proclaim this liberating news in word *and* deed.

Just As I Am, without One Plea:
One More Verse

The soul-seeking evangelist hogs center stage in Southern fiction's dramatization of Protestant religion. His excesses are what often cause critics to dismiss Christianity altogether, especially in the South. Readily identified and easily caricatured, the evangelist always calls out for "just one more verse" of the evangelical standard "Just As I Am, without One Plea." This view of the Southern evangelist suggests a mawkish traditionalism and increasing irrelevance of the church within contemporary culture. Perhaps we need the lampoon to help the church laugh at itself and, in the process, to clean up its own house.

Fiction such as O'Connor's and Hannah's, full of oddball characters and twisted plotlines, provokes us to reassess the place of evangelism within the Christian tradition. Their evangelists shout out the resilience of the gospel. They underscore the manifold personal and social illnesses that await the "refiner's fire" of gospel truth and the healing waters of Christian baptism. After all, the Great Commission of Matthew 28:18–20 gives the church its marching orders, whether we like it or not. The minister who moves about from place to place to announce the good news of Jesus Christ is not necessarily self-serving and hypocritical, though sometimes this is the case. Many evangelists do not fleece the flock. In faithfulness to their own conversion and call, and with sensitivity to the suffering of humanity, they point the alienated toward the healing grace of God and invite the lost to come home.

In fresh expressions of the Southern evangelical tradition of the revival, camp meetings, and spoken testimonies, the evangelist continues to ignite the flames of faith for new converts and stir up the dying embers of faith for those whose belief has grown cold. Rather than disappearing from contemporary religious life, the religious enthusiasm typically associated with the Protestant evangelist's work has, if anything, reemerged within North American Christianity among African American congregations and white evangelicals, albeit mostly outside of mainstream Protestant circles and no longer confined to the South. Those fictional evangelists who go beyond the stereotype show us complex characters whose religious zeal arises from the steadily burning conviction that one thing and one thing only matters: that everyone within earshot needs to hear that God through Jesus Christ has conquered sin and death, period. As Barry Hannah says about his own recent experience of encountering Christ, "I can doubt Him daily, hourly, but He will not fade from me."[17]

Evangelists like Summers and Byron Egan have undergone the brutal laceration of human sin (their own and others) and lived to tell about it. They are not attractive ministers. They will not serve the First Churches of the South. They have too many scars, hollowed-out eye sockets, tattoos, and spittle upon their collars. They are not hunting for the small game of petty sin and occasional lapses of clergy character, the vices that usually keep the church stirred up when it comes to clergy ethics. No, they are after much larger prey. They are tracking down the very forces of evil, the powers and principalities that rape human hope and devour charity. Thereby, they point us toward the renewal of Christian evangelism in a region that seems, when it comes to evangelism, to either prefer to live in the revival era past or the self-serving present.

Such notions of evangelism are disturbing. They suggest more conflict than many clergy and congregations are willing to take on. But that may be because we have mistaken small conflict in the church for the real deal. When ministers think that conflict in ministry is the occasional church spat over hymn selections or Sunday school curriculum, we are grossly mistaken. Byron Egan takes on no less than the entire gambling and prostitution industry. Both are contemporary forms of slavery of the desperate and weak. Both are forms of entertainment for the rich and powerful. In Egan's approach to evangelism, ministers should be leading spiritual combat with the "powers" and "principalities" of the universe (Romans 8:38; Ephesians 6:12 RSV). As Martin Luther expresses it, we fight "the prince of darkness grim" ("A Mighty Fortress"). The battle is not just for the individual soul of the believer, as in so much of Southern evangelical Protestantism, but for the soul of creation and the human race.

These Southern fried servings of the ministry upset and energize. On the one hand, the clergy of O'Connor and Hannah can keep ministers awake at night, wondering, What we have given our lives to? In the shadow of Bryon Egan pacing the rows of one-armed bandits at the casino, how important are those things that most of us as ministers spend our time doing? Do we really believe it is moral to lift the money from the working poor, as we do in legalized gambling and state-supported lotteries, and then give it back to the middle and upper classes in the form of tax rebates and scholarships for college education for the most gifted? How much more self-serving can we be? Is the house already on fire yet none of us are willing to see it? The early church father Chrysostom warned, "A fire is blazing in the roof of the church. Yet no one seems roused up by it." Have we become so stupefied by Western affluence that we look the other way as the poor stream into the gambling halls to toss away their last ten dollars? When prostitutes sell their bodies for one more needle and a shot of forgetfulness, does the church really care? And where will the warehousing of our elders end? Not the nice, posh, ultramodern retirement communities, where our affluent elderly continue to know "quality of life," but the squalid and cramped nursing homes of our inner cities and rural outposts, where the weakest and poorest of the elderly sleep the narcotic-induced and fetid sleep of zombies. Which way is ministry, then, when the most incisive writers splash these images upon the screens of our consciousness, or remind us that the images were already there, just in sleep mode? It disturbs us, and that is exactly what Bevel Summers and Byron Egan are intended to do.[18]

At the same time, these alarming fictional clergy compel. Whether backwoods prophet or reformed drug addict turned Baptist preacher, they point toward the high calling of Christian ministry. These clergy are edgy; in Christian terms, apocalyptic. They push toward a disastrously hopeful, God-blessed turn of events. Clergy and laity should read these novels with all the lights turned on.

In true evangelical fashion, these fictional evangelists first remind us, then tell us again, that all is not well in the South or anywhere else. Human beings are a sin-riddled lot, which Calvin reminded the church during the Reformation, a message that has been passed on to Southern religion through theological DNA. Sometimes we think that the South has traveled a great distance from its harshest sins of the past. But at other times, we see that our sin clings to us on every side. As Peter Applebome concludes about the South in his insightful book *Dixie Rising,*

> Looked at one way, it's a place of grace and faith that has purged most of its old sins while maintaining most of its old virtues, a place that

for all its bloody past and the ambiguities and unresolved issues of the present, offers the nation's best blueprint for racial peace. Looked at another way, it's a Potemkin village of mirrors and trap doors, where old inequities are cloaked in new forms, a chameleon South changed only on the surface, now pumping old poisons into new veins, a place where even in the most neutered suburbs, what was still lives, beating insistently away like Poe's telltale heart.

Ministers who are serious about the troubles of the day could learn a thing or two from O'Connor's Bevel Summers and Barry Hannah's Byron Egan. They remove the scales from our eyes and help us see the muck that accumulates like the dredges of Hurricane Katrina both inside and outside of the church. Many of the generational sins of the South, such as racism, remain embedded within church and culture, perhaps less obviously so and thereby even more corrosive of human well-being. So too Southern classism, which is equally if not more divisive today than racism. Church and society awaits clergy who, like Byron Egan, are not afraid to resist the powers that be.[19]

This leads to a final consideration of Egan. In him we see the blurring of the lines between the minister as evangelist and as pastor. While Egan's clearest call is to evangelize casino zombies and rescue abused children, he does so from the home base of a congregation, where he carries out the routine pastoral responsibilities of leading weekly worship and presiding over funerals. With tenderness he eulogizes a neighbor, "She lived a life that deserved a cathedral." Unlike O'Connor's Bevel Summers, Byron Egan becomes the pastor of those whom he evangelizes. He is disarmingly honest with the members of the church, sharing openly about his own addictions to cigarettes and hoping that his own struggles might be a witness to others. "Even with wrestling and prayer, even tears and spasms into the wee hours, he could not quit cigarettes. Maybe a sign to the weak ones they would be let in and forgiven too." He grafts his converts into a living body, a congregation, where they find belonging and a spiritual home.[20]

So in the middle of this wildly imaginative story, through a word-intoxicated and in-your-face evangelist, we find a realistic portrayal of the overlapping roles of the minister. The minister is not exclusively preacher or evangelist, pastor or administrator, but carries out each of these roles within the vocation of ministry as a whole. As raucous as Rev. Bryon Egan is as an evangelist, itching to square off with evil itself, he is also a pastor: one who gently invites the congregation to listen to God and one another, even to listen to the animals. As pastor, shepherd of the sheep, to be biblical about it, Egan is oddly Christlike. As Barry Hannah says, "Christ was tough, a calm but wild man." So with Egan pointing the way, we turn to the calmer yet complementary role of the clergy as pastor.[21]

4

Pour Out Your Hearts

The Minister as Pastor

Bess to repeat my position, let me state that I'm strongly in favor of prayer, but I feel what people really want is a medicine man, and I never rattle bones, do a rain dance, or wear chicken feathers.
—Wayland in William Hoffman's "The Question of Rain"

We use only first names in our place of worship. Last names remind us of the superficial—the world of wealth and connections and who came over on the Mayflower.
—Rev. Emmett to Ian in Anne Tyler's *Saint Maybe*

"Who could have invented a job called *pastor*?" Richard Lischer asks in his memoir, *Open Secrets*. For starters, the role binds the pastor into relationships and actions that few would undertake of their own volition: to care for the sick, comfort the bereaved, guide the perplexed, and reconcile the estranged. That means that pastors will spend more days than they can count hanging out in hospital rooms to pray with people who have medicine dripping into their arms from one bag and urine dripping from their bodies into another. They will huddle in dimly lit and overstuffed funeral parlors with shell-shocked parents who cannot begin to accept that the perfectly dressed and reposed body laying in the coffin is that of their dead daughter. They will counsel with a young man who desperately looks for strength to tell his family that he is homosexual, and they will labor to shore up a middle-aged couple whose marriage has all but washed away. On their behalf and for oneself, the pastor will hurl the words "My God, my God" into the darkness.[1]

These days of standing with others in their sorrow will alternate with days of celebration at births and baptisms, weddings and reunions. But the pastor who has been at it for a long time and who has a realistic understanding of human sin knows that even these joyful moments in ministry wind down or erupt into sorrow that requires a return to the shadows. The minister attempts to respond to all of this with the compassionate love of Christ—in biblical terms, to be a "shepherd" (pastor) of the congregation. It is a recipe for heartache followed by failure. Who,

43

except for one called by God, would do it? While the preacher and evangelist from the pulpit fulfill the public role of ordained ministry, the pastor moves more quietly within the living rooms, hospital corridors, and parking lots of the faithful to offer the tender care of Christ to specific human needs.

On the other hand, pastors are (or should be) suspicious of congregational "wants" and "needs." They recognize that genuine pastoral care is far more than holding hands and offering words of comfort, as important as that may be. God does not call the pastor to be "a quivering mass of availability," as Stanley Hauerwas puts it. Rather, as Eugene Peterson says, "Pastors are in charge of keeping the distinction between the world's lies and the gospel's truth clear." If all the congregation hears from the pastor is reinforcement of the world's lies—that life is about fulfillment of our own wants and needs—the pastor has swapped the demanding work of Christian soul care for the trivial tinkering of self-help therapy. A certain number within the congregation may want and need a pastor who always helps people "feel good about themselves." But the gospel names such desires a deception, and it points toward the surrender of self to Christ as the true road to wholeness. As Flannery O'Connor says, "That belief in Christ is to some a matter of life and death has been a stumbling block for readers who would prefer to think it a matter of no great consequence."[2]

The pastor who is worth her calling cares compassionately *and* truthfully for others. Sometimes she must treat and bind the wounds of the congregation, and sometimes she must lance the sore to allow for genuine healing. If pastors focus exclusively upon sustaining individuals or families who are passing through the jagged crises of life, pastoral care becomes truncated. This encourages dependency on the pastor and limits Christian ministry to triage or bedside care. Along that way in ministry lie the twin dangers of heroism and sentimentalism. Conversely, the pastor who indiscriminately brandishes the sword of truth in every pastoral situation will most likely maim the congregation, or pick some fights not worth winning. Along that way lie the dangers of self-righteousness and isolation. As difficult as it is, pastors who genuinely care for the congregation will try to strike a balance in ministry between tenderness and truthfulness. They may not succeed, but that doesn't excuse them from trying.

Like Jacob at the Jabbock, the pastors in Southern fiction wrestle with this complicated role of ministry. Some of them cannot maintain the balance between compassion and truth and fall off either on the side of sentimentality, like Father Tim in the novels of Jan Karon, or on the side of rigid adherence to principle, as in William Hoffman's short story "The Question of Rain." Then there are the fictional pastors who, like their real-life counterparts, try to provide pastoral care that is both compassionate and truthful, even if they do not always succeed. We will see one such pastor in Anne Tyler's novel *Saint Maybe*. These fictional ministers scatter light upon the pastor who seeks to provide the guiding, healing, sustaining, and reconciling love of God to church and community.

I'm Strongly in Favor of Prayer, but . . . :
Watering the Roots of Care
in William Hoffman's "The Question of Rain"

The request by a church member is so simple and straightforward that it catches the Presbyterian pastor, Wayland, off guard: "I'd like you to pray for rain." In fact, the whole congregation wants Wayland to pray for rain, the sooner the better. Without rain, the local knitting mills of this flat Virginia town near Danville might close because they depend upon an adequate water supply for the dye-making process; crops will wither in the fields of the Piedmont. Both scenarios forecast hardship for pastor Wayland's small-town, Southern congregation. They don't want him to pray for rain in general. With lawns "scorched right to the soil," they want Wayland to designate the upcoming Sunday service as a "Special Prayer Day for Rain." Thus begins Virginian William Hoffman's short story "The Question of Rain."[3]

Pastor Wayland finds himself smack dab in the middle of a pastoral dilemma that he'd much rather avoid. Helpless to change the drought, the congregation presses their pastor to intercede with God on behalf of the community. They have no qualms about making this specific request of God and the minister. They are willing to go on record with their hope that congregational prayer might sway the will of God. As one member says, "The more people we gather . . . in the church would appear to make praying more productive." The earnest appeal pushes Wayland into a corner where as pastor and theologian in residence he must explain theologically and pastorally why he will not lead such a worship service. "God knows our needs. He meets them out of His love for us. We don't pray to ask favors as if He's a rich uncle, but to have fellowship with Him, to achieve a feeling that we are close and in His care."

When a member persists, "Would it hurt to try?" Wayland continues to roll out his theological rationale for refusing the pastoral request.

> I don't suppose it could hurt anything. The question is whether or not our regular worship service ought to be used. I don't object to rain as part of the general prayer, but to make rain the point of an entire service not only might set a precedent whereby people would soon request snow on Christmas or cooling breezes in August. . . . He will order affairs so that we want nothing in any essential way.

Wayland's response is theologically sound. As a pastor within the Reformed tradition, he wants to direct the congregation toward praise of the almighty God rather than pestering God with trifling requests. As their pastor, he is willing to place before God the need for rain within the general needs of humanity, but Wayland will not lead a direct appeal. He believes that it is his pastoral responsibility to guard against approaching God, in Harry Emerson Fosdick's memorable phrase, like a "cosmic bellboy."[4]

At the root of this situation lies a familiar problem for pastor and congregation. The people experience a genuine need, in this case for something as elemental as rain. Since God as Creator is responsible for sun and rain, the people naturally turn to God when drought occurs. The pastor who truly cares for the people shares their need and understands their request. But as the resident pastor *and* theologian, he does not want to compromise theological integrity for the sake of congregational appeasement. As Wayland says to Caroline Devereaux when she states that she heard he was against it, "Against it, not you. Refusing you ladies anything distresses me. I'd rather suffer toads and boils. Yet I know you wouldn't want me to do something I consider wrong for myself and the church." At his lowest point, Wayland says, "I feel everybody in the country's taking a bite out of me."[5]

Sunday is approaching and Wayland cannot sidestep the concern. Does the pastor cave in to congregational petitions out of his love for the people, even if he believes that their theology is wrong? Or does he stand firm on the high ground of theological conviction while congregational resentment builds?

Wayland discovers a third option that has the ring of pastoral integrity: He listens. First, he listens to Carson Puckett, a respected patriarch of the congregation, a man "who could strike a rock for water, tread unravished among beasts." Puckett calmly says to Wayland, "I believe the Lord will give us rain if we ask for it. He'll find a way."

Because this affirmation comes from a member that the whole congregation respects, for the first time Wayland begins to see things from another angle. "Maybe I'm wrong. I could be behaving like one of these slick modern ministers who act as if Scriptures were private property. I've become so professional I've lost sight of the power of simple belief." Wayland hears in Carson Puckett not only the sounds of congregational need but also the sounds of congregational faith. Wayland is not the private security guard of theological truth. He is the pastor of the people whom God has entrusted to his care. They, too, know something about Christian faith, and through Carson Puckett they are beginning to educate their pastor.[6]

Second, he listens to his former seminary professor at Union Theological Seminary in Richmond. Wayland trusts Professor Koppman, who "believed the ministry was life's highest calling" and who "loved parable and paradox." When Wayland lays out his pastoral dilemma, Koppman whoops, "Oh brother, I'm glad it's you, not me. I'd rather be roasted over hot coals. Lord, deliver my heifers from the drought!"[7] When Wayland protests that the whole situation is not nearly as funny as Koppman thinks, the professor responds, "So you've come to a foolish professor in a preacher factory and want him to tell you what to do. Listen, the understanding of faith is not in the seminaries. Faith exists in the recesses of that mad place, the heart, and who knows the labyrinthine corridors of the heart?" Maybe, Wayland realizes, he is longing for the certainty of rules when genuine faith is always a risk.[8]

The conversation drives Wayland deeper into the territory of faith, closer to the mystery of God, where he must seek an answer to this pastoral dilemma. There will be no safe place to stand. At home in his study, Wayland prays, "Father, open me to Thy will so that what I do may be for Thy glory." Following this moment of surrender, and in solidarity with the community who has been placed on water restrictions, the pastor gives up his evening shower, edging closer to joining the congregation as their pastor.[9]

Wayland makes the final leap after a gentle nudge from Mims, his wife, who has supported him throughout the ordeal. He asks Mims about this congregation, whose desires have confounded him. "Who are they?" Her answer bridges the divide between pastor and people. "We can't expect them to be more than human." With this, Wayland sees the congregation, his pastoral role, and the place of prayer with the wonder of new sight. For a moment Wayland chastises himself for not seeing this simple truth earlier, yet he feels grateful that insight has finally come. He asks Mims, "Would you consider your husband a weak, spineless creature if he reversed himself and decided to hold the rain service?" To which Mims replies, naming the biblical significance of Wayland's reversal, "My husband, the good shepherd, wants to feed his flock."[10]

When Wayland comes around to embrace the congregation's desire for a prayer service for rain, he does so not out of compromise but out of a deeper appreciation for the congregation's humanity. With the help of wise friends, he climbs off the rock of theological assurance into the barren place of human longing, from where he can make an intercessory appeal on their behalf. Now he stands with the people, not as a high priest but as one who intercedes on their behalf, trusting as they must in God's mercy, for they have nowhere else to turn (Hebrews 4:14–16). The congregation has broken through to Wayland to remind him that in his pastoral vocation he stands with them as one in Christ. They pour their own humanity upon the pastor to water his parched roots of care—because, as Mims says, they can't be more than they are: human. So, the newly baptized pastor prays for the rain that they all need.

We should not be surprised that when the story concludes, watery thunderheads begin to form and pour "slashing, luminous rain" upon the community. Humbled and renewed in his faith, Wayland responds appropriately with "gratitude [that] brought him near to weeping."[11]

In Presbyterian pastor Wayland, we find a reliable minister with a believable pastoral dilemma. Wayland wrestles with self, congregation, and God in a manner that edifies pastoral ministry. In the parched congregation's pleas for rain, Wayland finally recognizes that theological integrity is not at stake; the caring relationship between the pastor and congregation is. They simply want a pastor to lead them in prayers, not to speak beyond them or outside of them but for them. Pastor Wayland discovers that some occasions call for theological tough-mindedness while others urge gentle compassion. It is the lot of the caring pastor to figure out the difference.

Pastoral care is not something that ministers accomplish while gardening alone. Failure to connect with others has always been a hazard in ministry. Sentimentalism or rigidity threatens to undermine pastoral care at every turn. It's understandable that pastors want easy solutions to complex human problems. And when those solutions are not found, the pastor may withdraw in discouragement and substitute thinking about pastoral care for actually doing it. "I know I need to go to see Mr. Clayton; he's so lonely," the pastor says to himself. "Maybe next week after I get the shut-in list typed up in this new database." The temptation must be resisted. As difficult as it is, pastoral care cannot occur without truly engaging human suffering within the church and world. It is accomplished by actually listening, talking, and praying with others in the name of Jesus Christ.

"A Question of Rain" soaks ministers with the awareness that the incarnation of God through Jesus Christ is the basis of genuine pastoral care. It reminds us that the only place pastoral care can possibly occur is within human communities, in communities where drought and rain are not abstract terms of theological riddles but the substance of life. These are real flesh-and-blood communities with people worth caring about and something worth praying for.

We Use Only First Names in Our Place of Worship: Bearing Mutual Burdens in Anne Tyler's *Saint Maybe*

Anne Tyler is a long-term resident of Baltimore, where *Saint Maybe* and much of her fiction is set. Baltimore's identity, like Tyler's, straddles the North and South. In this novel, nevertheless, Tyler's preoccupation with conservative Protestant evangelicalism—including its revival-shaped hymnody, emphasis on personal salvation, focus on family relations over time, and the influence of the past on the present and future—mark the work as thematically Southern. The Baltimore of the 1960s, when this story takes place, has a distinctively small Southern city "feel"—like a Jacksonville, Savannah, or Knoxville—especially a Southern city before the Sun Belt boom of the 1970s.[12]

It is in this northernmost reach of the South, Baltimore, where the novel's protagonist, seventeen-year-old Ian Bedloe, lives. Ian is the youngest of three children, and they are Waverly Street's version of the "ideal, apple-pie household: two amiable parents, three good looking children, a dog, a cat, a scattering of goldfish."[13] Ian, a bright student who does not apply himself in school, is an outstanding pitcher for the Poe High School team. As Presbyterians, the Bedloes attend church sporadically and look to the minister for presiding at family weddings and funerals. All is well within the Bedloe world until Ian's brother, Danny, is killed in a car wreck.[14]

Danny's death throws the family into a crisis, especially young Ian, who is convinced that he is responsible for it, because he meddled too much in the marriage of Danny and Lucy, a waitress and not quite in the Bedloe's social class. Ian believes that by planting suspicion in Danny's mind about Lucy's marital fidelity, he caused Danny to snap and "accidentally" commit suicide by crashing his car into a retaining wall. He attempts to suppress his guilt, but it will not let him go.

> He would see it looming in his path . . . and all at once it would rise up in front of him: *Danny is dead. He died. Died. . . .* And then a thought that was even worse: *He died on purpose. He killed himself.* And finally the most horrible thought of all: *Because of what I told him.*

Ian finds temporary solace at the funerals of Danny and later of Lucy, who dies after delivering Danny's child. But the balm of the funeral liturgy is short-lived for Ian, who now also feels responsible for the lives of the three children that Danny and Lucy left behind. It is a crushing load of responsibility and "anguish over something impulsively done that could not be undone" for Ian. If anyone ever needed a pastor, it's Ian.[15]

Ian meets Rev. Emmett on a dismal January evening when walking home from work through downtown Baltimore. The meeting will turn Ian's life around. On impulse, he stops and enters the downtown Baltimore storefront CHURCH OF THE SECOND CHANCE where a Wednesday evening prayer service is under way. Inside, Ian encounters a congregation of fifteen or twenty people singing "Blessed Jesus! Blessed Jesus!" in an affectionate way that "sounded personally welcoming." Rev. Emmett, "a tall, black-haired man in a tieless white shirt and black trousers," presides over the prayer service. He welcomes friends "and guests" and then extends the invitation to congregational prayer by saying, "We have reached that point in the service when any person here is invited to step forward and ask for our prayers. No request is too great, no request is trivial in the eyes of God our Father." In response, members of the congregation begin to offer their petitions, one for a friend with diabetes, and another for a grieving mother whose son has been killed in the Vietnam War. Each petition is followed by sustained silence that Ian realizes is a planned part of the service. "The minister stood with both palms raised, his face tipped skyward and his eyelids closed and gleaming. . . . For our sister, Clarice," the minister prays. These are heartfelt prayers uttered out of personal loss. Rev. Emmett receives each prayer with pastoral sensitivity and lifts the request to God in silence.[16]

The simplicity of the setting, the sincerity of the people, and the patience of the pastor draw Ian in. Before he can stop himself, Ian is on his feet, pouring out his feelings of unworthiness before a room full of strangers and a spiritually perceptive pastor.

> "I used to be good," he said. "Or I used to be not bad, at least. Not evil. I just *assumed* I wasn't evil, but lately, I don't know what happened. Everything I touch goes wrong. . . . Pray for me to be good again," he told them. "Pray for me to be forgiven."

As with the others who have sought prayer, when Ian sits down, Rev. Emmett raises his palms and bids the congregation to pray in silence. The silence is like a whispered promise to Ian of the possibility of forgiveness. Following this prayer for Ian, the service concludes with the singing of the standard evangelical hymn "Leaning on the Everlasting Arms."[17]

Everything else that transpires flows from this one moment in worship. A young man bearing a burden of guilt finds the beginning of release, not from friends and family, and not from his own congregation's minister, but from a storefront minister and nondenominational congregation who practice the Christian virtue of mutual burden bearing. Pastoral care, in this case, begins in worship rather than in the counseling session or private confessional. Though it takes Ian a while to figure things out, he has stumbled upon a minister and a Christian congregation who recognize that worship is where God's care is first made known. Worship is where believers take the first step of converting holy words into truthful deeds. Rev. Emmett's straightforward leadership of congregational prayers becomes the first key to unlock Ian's guilt and grief and signals for him a new direction in life. Rev. Emmett proves Elaine Ramshaw's claim that "presiding at worship is the paradigmatic act of pastoral care." All other acts of pastoral care take their direction from worship, where the needs of the individual and congregation are joined to the presence of God through prayer, hymn, the sharing of God's word, and the breaking of bread. Having praised God and received God's goodness in worship, the believers are sent into the world, equipped to live faithfully.[18]

In his final act of liturgical pastoral care for the evening, Rev. Emmett announces, "Go ye now into the world and bear witness to His teachings. In Jesus' name, amen."[19] And here is where his pastoral care becomes noteworthy. Ian asks for prayers from this well-meaning Christian congregation, and they answer his request with genuine Christian concern. In many congregations, Ian might now be left alone to return to his family on Waverly Street and decide for himself what to do with this religious *experience*. But this will not do for Rev. Emmett and the Church of the Second Chance. A wise spiritual guide who is willing to take initiative, Rev. Emmett will not allow Ian to depart the service and remain wrapped in his own private experience. "I hope your prayer was answered this evening," he says to Ian as they get ready to leave. When Ian fumbles for an appropriate reply, Emmett presses. "But your prayer. Was there any response?" The pastor will not accept Ian's vagueness. His forthrightness is disarming. "What was it that you needed forgiven?"[20]

With this direct inquiry, pastoral care of Ian reaches a critical moment. Ian can either embrace Rev. Emmett's invitation for full confession or he can cut and run.

> Ian couldn't believe his ears. Was this even legal, inquiring into a person's private prayers? He ought to spin on his heel and walk out. But instead . . . In a voice not quite his own, he said, "I caused my brother to, um, kill himself. . . . I told him his wife was cheating on him, . . . and now I'm not even sure she was. . . . I know I wasn't *totally* wrong, but . . . So he drove into a wall. And then his wife died of sleeping pills, and I guess you could say I caused that too, more or less."

As Ian lays out his burdensome story, Rev. Emmett listens attentively. He does not interrupt or press for details. He does not try to console Ian prematurely or seek to reframe the story, as some pastors might. He simply waits until Ian stops to seek pastoral confirmation of his own forgiveness.

> So anyhow, that's why I asked for that prayer. And I honestly believe it might have worked. Oh, it's not like I got an answer in plain English, of course, but . . . don't you think? Don't you think I'm forgiven?

Ian lays bare his heart to the pastor, pours out his own sin real or imagined and awaits absolution. Reverend Emmett's response could not be more unexpected.

> "Goodness, no," Reverend Emmett said briskly.
> Ian's mouth fell open. He wondered if he'd misunderstood. He said, "I'm *not* forgiven?"
> "Oh, no."
> "But . . . I thought that was kind of the point," Ian said. "I thought God forgives everything."
> "He does," Reverend Emmett said. "But you can't just say, 'I'm

sorry, God.' Why, anyone could do that much! You have to offer reparation—concrete, practical reparation, according to the rules of the church."[21]

Pastors who wonder what to do after we say "Your sins are forgiven" should take note of this scene. Reverend Emmett will not dispense cheap grace to Ian. Emmett sees that what Ian needs is not a papering over of his offense but a disciplined response to the guilt and grief. When Ian asks what if his offense is something that reparations will not fix, Rev. Emmett elaborates. "Well, that's where Jesus comes in, of course . . . . Jesus remembers how difficult life on earth can be. He helps with what you can't undo. But only after you've *tried* to undo it." Ian quickly figures out that in Rev. Emmett he has met a pastor who will not give him what he wants but what he needs. When Rev. Emmett suggests that Ian must assume the responsibility for his brother's children, "to lean into his burden," Ian asks in exasperation, "What kind of cockeyed religion *is* this?" To which Rev. Emmett replies, "It's the religion of atonement and complete forgiveness. It's the religion of the Second Chance." This bracing pastoral conversation concludes with Ian looking at Rev. Emmett and observing that "he had never seen anyone so absolutely at peace." On his way home Ian understands what Rev. Emmett meant when he said in their initial introductions, "We use only first names in our place of worship. Last names remind us of the superficial."[22]

Reverend Emmett's pastoral care of Ian is anything but superficial. It will seem presumptuous to some readers, and especially in an era that holds religious privacy as inviolate, his actions seem inexcusably intrusive. For those who think that pastoral counseling consists of little more than nondirective listening, Emmett's direct advice is heavy-handed. Leaving Ian to figure out his own problems and devise his own solutions is exactly what has landed him in the mess that he is in. Ian does not need more time to think things out for himself or to pretend, as his family has done for so many years, that "everything is alright."

The fact is that Ian did play a part in his brother's death. Some kind of atonement appears to be necessary in his case, and Emmett is pastor enough to recognize that an easy pronunciation of forgiveness will not suffice. Ian needs authentic Christian community and accountability in order to lay hold of the grace of God that will free him from the inner torment of sin and that will keep him in communion with his own family. Reverend Emmett does not want to be Ian's psychological counselor.

Rather, he represents for the boy both God's grace and God's demand. In order to "help" Ian, he must tell Ian the truth—God's truth—as best he understands it, and thereby provide spiritual guidance for Ian. Reverend Emmett functions as "curate," the curer of souls, and there is nothing easy about the responsibility.

Reverend Emmett's pastoral theology appears to be long on works and short on grace. On the one hand, it cuts against the grain of a religiously sentimental culture that has all but washed sin from its vocabulary. North American Christians are by and large unwilling to hold one another accountable for any sort of moral failure even though a rhetoric of personal righteousness dominates the booming conservatism of evangelical preachers and elected officials. When it comes to personal and public morality, a glaring double standard is at work in which the louder the church and state decry "sin," the more we seem to look the other way when it lands on our own doorsteps. What else would explain the anomaly that the South, the Bible Belt, where politicians and ministers most consistently tout "family values," has the highest divorce rate in the country? Reverend Emmett's pastoral care disturbs because he actually expects that if Ian is really contrite, he will do something about his offense. "God wants to know how far you'll go to undo the harm you've done," Rev. Emmett says. Many pastors would back away from making such an audacious claim, but Rev. Emmett means it.[23]

Reverend Emmett's pastoral care also disturbs because it flirts with the sin of works righteousness that the entire Protestant Reformation sought to correct through recovery of the biblical principle of *sola gratia*. To be sure, a strain of works righteousness runs through Rev. Emmett's ministry that is potentially troublesome. Taken to extremes, it can lead to a tyranny of the law. Yet Rev. Emmett has spotted the moral vacuum of North America's at-ease religious culture; he will not worship at its altar. Reverend Emmett is the exact opposite of the minister of a mainline Protestant church that Ian visits, where "the pastor—a slouching, easygoing, just-one-of-the guys type with a sweater vest showing beneath his suit coat—counseled his listeners to be kind to themselves, to take time for themselves in the midst of the hurly-burly." The sermon and service leave Ian with "enormous yawns hollowing the back of his throat." Such a pastor cannot possibly lead Ian to the healing waters of salvation.[24]

The gospel of Jesus Christ, as Rev. Emmett sees it, means nothing if it fails to change (convert) a person's life, to reorient the believer to a new reality, the resurrected Christ, and to shape the believer around a new set of values that are often in tension with the values of culture. This is why he leads Ian and the members of the congregation to gather monthly on Saturdays to "do good works" for each other and for strangers in the community. The church members believe that their "lives are a missionary outreach" within culture. This is why the members of the church take vows to abstain from those things that will harm the body such as alcohol, caffeine, and even sugar. Emmett tries to establish moral principles for the congregation within a relativistic and suicidal culture. He does so out of concern to edify a congregation that has something worthwhile to share with the world. While he seeks to provide wise pastoral guidance for the church, Rev. Emmett never believes that he has all the answers. And as shepherd of the congregation, he leads with humility, "remarkably unimpressed with his own importance."[25]

In the end, Rev. Emmett leads Ian to the startling and grace-filled liberation of the gospel. After years of faithfulness, following through on his commitment to raise Danny and Lucy's children, Ian still struggles to know forgiveness. The burden will not let him rest. He pushes Rev. Emmett: "How much longer till I'm forgiven?" But Emmett recognizes that Ian's burden is not because he sinned against his brother and his brother's wife. Rather, Ian's sin is that of being unwilling to forgive them for having died, for having left him with so much responsibility. "The burden," Emmett says, "is that *you* must forgive." With this spiritual guidance, something begins to move within Ian. He is "acutely conscious all at once of motion, of flux and possibility . . . He believed that he would get there [to God] in the end."[26] After all, as the book concludes, in the subtle way that God works through others, like Ian, like Rev. Emmett, like the "sisters and brothers" who form the Church of the Second Chance, "people changed other people's lives every day of the year. There was no call to make such a fuss about it."[27]

Reverend Emmett is a pastor who serves as a physician of the soul and as moral guide. He presides over a nondenominational urban outpost of Christianity that cuts against the grain of Southern establishment Christianity. He's edgy; he makes us squirm. Reverend Emmett dares to meddle. He is honest with others and himself, and he expects accountability among the members who call each other "Brother" and "Sister." Such accountability in North American Christianity is rare these days, perhaps most rare in a Southern culture where social graces still dictate that everyone must pretend to get along. Ian Bedloe can become a "Saint Maybe" because his pastor and congregation provide him enough guidance in the practice of the Christian virtues—especially the virtues of forgiveness,

charity, and humility—that they can begin to take hold in his life. Growing into the fullness of Christ will take a lifetime and beyond, but with
the guidance of Rev. Emmett and the prayers of the saints, by the story's
end Ian is well on his way.

Pastor: Formed and Reformed

The Christian minister as pastor is a complex figure whose depth Southern fiction writers do not frequently plumb. Clyde Edgerton, for example, who tends to satirize his fictional ministers, once remarked that the
more he edited the religious characters in his stories, the more he tried
to make them sympathetic and humane. But the fact is, the pastor is
easier to satirize or sentimentalize than to portray with the full complement of characteristics that do justice to the role. Fortunately, some
writers such as William Hoffman in "The Question of Rain" and Anne
Tyler in *Saint Maybe* do manage to depict the minister as pastor in a way
that vivifies the image.[28]

Such well-rounded pastors in Southern fiction instruct as much by
their shortcomings as by their strengths. When suffering or moral failure take up residence with the Christian pastor, as they will surely do,
and the pastor manages to survive without losing all faith, then the person who emerges on the other side usually has something worthwhile
to report to other believers, whether he is still an ordained minister or
not. They have become Christian persons and pastors who are formed
and reformed.

Pastors are never fixed once and for all as a person or as an ordained
minister. They move through the seasons of life just like all other Christians, aware that the Spirit of God can use all of life's blessings and sor-
rows to shape and reshape them as followers of Jesus Christ. When
suffering or failure becomes the shaping force, then the faithful pastor
will pray for endurance that might convert wounds into redemptive
scars. Of course, as one of Doris Betts's characters says, "a flood of suffering [does] not always leave behind an unexpected high-water mark
of good." But for many pastors in fiction and reality, trouble becomes
the doorway to a new faith where, like Pastor Wayland in William Hoffman's short story, the pastor is able to more fully bless the humanity of
others.[29]

To return to a point made earlier, one thing that most faithful pastors share is the close connection between their pastoral care and their

leadership of worship. For both William Hoffman's Pastor Wayland and Anne Tyler's Rev. Emmett, their role as worship leader gives direction to their pastoral care. In the case of Pastor Wayland, the congregation's need for intercessory prayer in corporate worship serves as a refining fire for his pastoral care. For Rev. Emmett, Ian's hunger for confession, penance, and absolution comes to light when the congregation gathers to pray. Neither of these pastoral care concerns would even emerge if the ordained minister were not the one to whom the congregation looks to preside over worship. As Will Willimon puts it, "Laypersons . . . know enough to sense that if the pastor cannot be helpful to them in the leadership of the community's worship, the pastor will not be of much help to them elsewhere." In the life of the minister, the links between pastoral care, worship leadership, and preaching cannot be severed. Each role gives theological purpose and practical direction to the other. Phillips Brooks said in his Lyman Beecher Lectures, "The preacher who is not a pastor grows remote; the pastor who is not a preacher grows petty." Whether thinking about it formally or not, those Southern fiction writers, such as Hoffman and Tyler, who understand that pastoral care and worship go hand in hand, are the ones who offer portraits of ministry that are lively enough to arrest our attention and complex enough to instruct.[30]

The pastor who encourages the believers to "pour out your hearts" to God is also the priest who invites the congregation to "lift up your hearts" in praise and adoration. The one who listens to a parishioner puzzle over a personal dilemma on Friday is the one who serves bread and wine at the altar table on Sunday. The one who prays in the middle of the night with a brokenhearted wife in the hospital is the one who proclaims "Christ is risen" in the front of the sanctuary. If not for the altar and sanctuary where the good news of God is proclaimed and received, how could the pastor possibly go to the home and hospital when bad news breaks? She does not show up as pastor alone but also as priest, to mediate God's grace through Jesus Christ to all the saints. So we turn now from pastor to the corresponding image of the minister as priest in Southern literature.

5

Lift Up Your Hearts

The Minister as Priest

Are you a psychiatrist or a priest or a priest-psychiatrist? Frankly, you remind me of something in between, one of those failed priests who go into social work or "counseling," or one of those doctors who suddenly decides to go to the seminary. Neither fish nor fowl.
—Lance Lamar to Father John in Walker Percy's *Lancelot*

Most of them call me Pastor Margaret. It's a form just coming into use in our church that we all feel comfortable with. . . . One time a little boy who was visiting called me Father—because of the vestments, I guess. But I wish you'd call me Margaret.
—Pastor Margaret Bonner to Helen Britt in Gail Godwin's *Evensong*

In many quarters of the overwhelmingly Protestant South, the term "priest" still registers as exotic. And if not exotic, then, different. As the writer Pat Conroy recalls, "Being Catholic in the South was the weirdest thing one could be when I was growing up." And as historian Samuel Hill observes, "Most considered [Catholicism] no Christianity at all and beyond that a menace to all things noble." "Preacher Smith," "Pastor Matthews," "Brother Lloyd," and "Sister Bessie" belong in the Southern religious tent, we know. But "Father Callahan and his followers"? Many Southerners are not sure.[1]

There are exceptions. The closer you get to Louisiana with its jambalaya heritages of Native American, West Indian, African, French Canadian, Italian, Irish, Spanish, and British, the more frequently you see the spires of Catholic cathedrals and the artifacts of the African ancestral religions. Along the Texas-Mexico border and throughout southern Florida, you frequently see Catholic Parish signboards announcing "Misa" and hear Hispanic Americans addressing their religious leader as "Padre." Somewhere in most Southern towns, there's a modest Catholic Church open for mass, and in many cities a cathedral with a full complement of worship services, parochial schools, and social outreach. At the center of each of these presides the priest.[2]

The other "priests" of the South, the Episcopalians, fare better in terms of social acceptance; although they hold only a small minority of adherents in the South, the economic status of their membership coupled with the historical significance of many Southern Episcopalians secures an influence on Southern culture not afforded the Catholics. To be sure, the stereotyped genteel refinement of the Episcopal priest is occasionally parodied and frequently misunderstood by the evangelical Southern Baptist or Pentecostal, and this is picked up in some fiction. In Clyde Edgerton's *Raney*, for example, the Southern Baptist Raney, whose husband Charles is an Episcopalian, challenges him about his denomination: "They're against some of the things we believe in most. . . . They serve real wine at the Lord's Supper. And they have priests, don't they?" Still, this is not the same kind of distrust directed at the Catholic priest in the South.[3]

But the sectarian use of the term "priest" to designate either the Roman Catholic or Episcopal ordained is not the whole story. For the ordained minister, Protestant or Catholic, engages in priestly action all the time. The minister functions as priest when he presides in worship through leading the public prayers of petition, confession, and absolution and when he administers the sacraments. The ministers serve a priestly role when, through holy listening, she allows the guilty to lay down their burdens and receive the renewing grace of Christ. She provides spiritual direction for those whose faith has gone awry or who seek Christ-centered companionship to take the next steps in belief. The minister fulfills his priestly calling when he stands at the altar with a man and woman and unites them in a marriage covenant. At the graveside, the minister as priest leads the grieving congregation through the ancient ritual of Christian burial and proclaims the power of the resurrecting God. In all these ways, whether Baptist or Episcopal, Pentecostal or Roman Catholic, the minister fulfills the work of the priest within the community.

We will look at two ministers from Southern fiction who actually bear the title of priest: Father John in Walker Percy's *Lancelot* and Rev. Margaret Bonner in Gail Godwin's *Evensong*. But, as I've suggested, the priestly role extends to Christian ministry as a whole, even to those decidedly anti-Catholic Protestant ministers who wouldn't in a million years think of themselves as priests. As Luther phrased it so well, "As many of us as have been baptized are all priests without distinction, as indeed we all are. Yet to some has been committed public ministry with our consent."[4]

I Could Not Have Told Anyone Else:
Confessing Madness in Walker Percy's *Lancelot*

Walker Percy's *Lancelot* draws readers into a contemporary heart of darkness where madness and evil run amok. The heart and mind belong to the once-genteel Southern Louisiana aristocrat Lancelot (Lance) Andrewes Lamar. From his cell-like room in a New Orleans Center for Aberrant Behavior, he relates his tale of sexually charged murder and destruction. By the end of the story, the impotent Lance—self-professed "half-assed lawyer," a "moderate liberal, a moderate music lover, a moderate hunter and fisherman, and past president of the United Way," who spends most of his middle-aged days sitting in a rocking chair in the study of the antebellum Belle Isle Estate—has murdered his wife and her movie star lover and burned the Estate house to the ground. The story takes place sometime during the Nixon administration. The newspaper headlines scream out the horrific climax of Lance's drama: BELLE ISLE BURNS. BODIES OF FILM STARS CHARRED BEYOND RECOGNITION. SCION OF OLD FAMILY CRAZED BY GRIEF AND RAGE. SUFFERS BURNS TRYING TO SAVE WIFE.[5]

As is often the case, Lance's insanity masks extraordinary intelligence. As readers we cannot simply dismiss him as "criminally insane." His sickness is extreme, but it also indicates an astute person who has foundered upon the shoals of late modernity. As a Percy critic, John Desmond, points out, "Lance may well commit violent and perverted deeds, but for all that, he is, like Conrad's Mr. Kurtz [*Heart of Darkness*], a representative figure of the age, the 'age of interest.' Lance is "us," in extremis, as we see when he comments bitterly but perceptively on the state of Southern culture.

> The Southerner? The Southerner started out a skeptical Jeffersonian and became a crooked Christian. That is to say, he is approaching and has almost reached his essence, which is to be more crooked and Christian than ever before. Do you want a portrait of the New Southerner? He is Billy Graham on Sunday and Richard Nixon the rest of the week. He calls on Jesus and steals, he's in business, he's in politics.

Although more than a touch of paranoia lurks under these comments, they suggest a formidable intelligence and a keen social eye. His sardonic wit causes others to sit up and take notice.[6]

The character who illumines our inquiry into the priestly ministry is the one who listens to Lance Lamar's Gothic story, the Catholic priest-psychiatrist Father John. Chaplain of the institution, Father John visits Lance in the hospital. An old family friend and high school classmate, Father John converted from Protestantism to Roman Catholicism and became a priest. Their shared history in New Orleans provides a point of contact for the deranged Lance. "We were best of friends," Lance says, "in fact inseparable if you recall. It's just that it was quite a shock seeing you after all these years." With the trust implied by their shared past, Lance decides that he will talk to Father John.

> You're the first person I've wanted to see. I've refused all psychiatrists, ministers, priests, group therapy, and whatnot. . . . No, what first struck me about you was that you're the only person around here who doesn't want to talk.

Lance can at least partially see himself through Father John: "But when I saw you yesterday, it was like seeing myself. I had the sense of being overtaken by something, by the past, by myself." In other words, Father John, the priest counselor, provides a good-enough mirror for the chaotic Lance to see reflections of himself. Or to shift the therapeutic metaphor, Father John is a safe container for Lance's story. Lance implicitly trusts the priest to safely "hold" the fragments of the story while he (Lance) attempts to piece things together again.[7]

The relationship between Lance and the priest, however, goes beyond therapeutic transference. To Lance, Father John's identity is mixed and confusing, half priest and half psychiatrist, so he mocks the priest's turn to the psychotherapeutic.

> Well, I found out who you are. Your profession, that is. A priest-physician. Which is to say, a screwed-up priest or a half-assed physician. Or both. Ah, I managed to surprise you, didn't I?[8]

His skepticism suggests that a theological quest stirs beneath Lance's psychosocial trauma. Anton Boisen, the early-twentieth-century pioneer of the religion and mental health movement, argued that all mental struggle is at root a religious struggle. Though Lance is combative, he yearns for a spiritual guide who can help him find his way out of his internal chaos to reestablish human communion. As priest, Father John offers the possibility of religious hope for Lance, but as a psychiatrist he muddies the waters. Lance's caustic comments challenge the priest to claim his vocational identity as a priest of God and Jesus Christ. The real struggle and possible resolution will occur at the theological level.[9]

Father John accepts the challenge. Rather than attempt to psychoanalyze Lance, he listens to Lance's story as informal confession. "Come in, come in. . . . I have a confession to make," Lance says at their second encounter. Though later Lance protests that he has nothing to confess, it is clear that the entire murderous story is a confession, an attempt to find relief from his suffering and a bid for reconciliation. After the murder, after his vilifying of women, church, and culture, after a complete break with all those whom he loves and a fascist attempt at self-justification, Lance wants to tell his story to the priest, to purge himself of sin and evil and begin again.[10]

Father John fulfills his priestly role toward Lance through the tradition of holy listening. He rarely speaks. Indeed, until the very end of the novel, we only know of Father John's responses as they are echoed in the monologue of Lance Lamar. For example, Lance says, "You were asking me how I felt when I discovered Margot had been unfaithful to me." As readers we infer Father John's comments and reactions from the words of Lance. But the priest emerges as a quiet, almost-hidden presence as he receives the story. His spiritual guidance is indirect, gently inquiring. He nondefensively absorbs Lance's venom while containing his confusion. As Percy himself writes, "In such times, when everyone is saying 'Come!' it may well be that the best way to say 'Come!' is to remain silent."[11]

But it is at the deepest symbolic level—the sacramental—that the priest's ministry bears most significance. In a Southern culture where religion is frequently an exercise in word bombardment, ministers can learn from the silence of Father John. As priest and representative of God, Father John's presence "speaks" even though his words are absent. The priest has little to say because he stands as a silent, God-bearing witness to the torment of Lance's spirit. Precisely because Lance's rage at God, the church, women, and culture cannot drive Father John away, he signifies the possibility of a redemptive communion between humans and God. Though Lance denies that reconciliation is ever possible, Father John's constancy suggests otherwise. Though Lance drains the sacrament of holy communion of all divine mystery, Father John remains a "living reminder" that God through Christ joins human flesh.[12]

The incarnation of God in Jesus Christ affirms that as humans we are not simply spirits or bodies, but spirited bodies, whole selves made for love and communion with God *and* each other. To treat one another as mere objects for personal gratification (as with pornography) is no better or worse than withdrawing from one another into spiritual isolation (as with Gnosticism). Lance's madness is that of the modern age, which dualistically splits body from spirit and leaves us either rutting around in materialism or wafting away into spiritualism. Father John, by his silent yet compassionate presence within the prison of Lance's world, re-presents the whole truth—that in Christ, God is reconciling the world, flesh and all (2 Corinthians 5:19). Such is the sacramental significance of the one who wears the robe and collar.

By the end of the story, one thing is clear: Father John has reclaimed his primary vocational identity as priest. During their lengthy conversations, he has undergone transformation. We get the first clear evidence of Father John's transformation when in response to one of the many accusations that Lance hurls against the church—"I might have tolerated you and your Catholic Church, and even joined it, if you had remained true to yourself. Now you're part of the age"—he shows up the next day wearing his clerical garments. "How come you're wearing your priest uniform today?" Lance taunts. "Are you girding for battle or dressed up like Lee for the surrender?" Lance is correct. Father John has dressed up for battle—battle against the powers and principalities, the forces of darkness of the age that have swallowed up Lance Lamar. The terms of the struggle, sin versus grace, are clarified when Father John enters the cell as priest rather than as priest-psychiatrist. He brings to the battle the Christly sword of redemptive love symbolized in his vocational garments and embodied in his personhood. If communion is available for this monstrously errant knight, it will only come through the One that Father John, the priest, represents: Christ, the sacrament of God.[13]

Clarified by their encounter, Father John will leave the work of institutional chaplaincy and return to parish ministry. Lance confirms Father John's decision: "So you plan to take a little church in Alabama, Father, preach the gospel, turn bread into flesh, forgive the sins of Buick dealers, administer communion to suburban housewives?" This is exactly what Father John plans to do. He knows now that his priestly authority is grounded in Christ rather than social science and medicine. His ordination is to preach the gospel and confer the grace of Christ through daily communion with ordinary people in an ordinary place.[14]

As so often happens in Christian ministry, there are no startling resolutions to the drama that unfolds between Lance, Father John, and the silent but present God. Either Lance is correct and God is void, or Father John is correct and God is known in the daily communion between human beings infused with the sacramental presence of Christ. As Lance says, "One of us is wrong. It will be your way or it will be my way." To which Father John replies a simple, profound "Yes." For now, finally, at the end of the story, Father John speaks. But his only word is the repeated affirmation "Yes," "Yes," "Yes." More than any exquisite theological discourse, more than any apologetic for God in response to Lance's negations, Father John's "Yes" communicates the divine affirmation of grace. The final word of the story is not Lance's pounding "No" but Father John's quiet "Yes." The ending of this story suggests that maybe now, after all of Lance Lamar's manic ranting, he is ready to hear a word from God and receive the gift of grace mediated through the minister as priest.[15]

In Father John we see a subtle yet sure image of the Christian minister as priest. Whatever else the ministry entails, from preaching to evangelism and congregational administration to pastoral care, Father John recalls the central conviction of the church, both Protestant and Catholic, that the ordained minister represents Christ. While the Catholic Church understands the ministry itself as sacramental in an official sense, the conviction is not far from traditional Protestant understandings of ordination either. Yes, the Protestant understanding of ministry is broadly functional, with the ordained minister carrying out specialized and representative functions on behalf of the congregation. But the Protestant ministry is also deeply symbolic as the minister mediates between God and the people. As Calvin explains in his catechism, "To what is the office of priest conducive? First by means of it he is the mediator who reconciles us to the Father; and, secondly, access is given us to the Father, so that we too can come with boldness into his presence, and offer him the sacrifice of ourselves, and our all."[16]

In person and office the minister signifies Christ, the one who goes between God and humanity. This is just as true in the Protestant South as in any other region of the country. Why else would Protestant laity routinely ask their ministers to "pray for us"? What else could more fully explain the talismanic treatment Protestant ministers receive from their congregations? They put him on a pedestal, guard their speech, keep him at arm's distance until crisis erupts, and then summon him for constant intercessory prayer, counseling, and reading of Scriptures—in short, to be their bridge to God. In these ways, even the most sectarian and evangelical of the Southern Protestant ministers fulfill the ministry as priest every bit as much as their Catholic counterpart.

For those Protestant ministers who yearn for renewed contact with their own priestly calling, *Lancelot*'s Father John offers a whispered invitation. Though cultural chaos roars around us, our identity is quietly announced by bread and wine, basin and towel. As priests, we can trust that our vocation is much larger than ourselves. Wearing the yoke of Christ, his presence speaks through us, frequently through our own silent witness to him in the face of unmitigated suffering and evil. What minister has not tiptoed into an ICU unit where the pain is so horrific that words will only trivialize the situation? Who in ministry has not stumbled into the halls of nursing homes or mental health "asylums" and been struck dumb by the force of neglect and madness? In these situations, the words of the preacher must give way to the sacred symbols of the priest. Catholic or Protestant, the priest signals the loving "yes" of God to the people and places who are otherwise ruled by destruction. Maybe in the South, where too often in ministry we hurl words like weapons, yet to no avail, it is time to trust the sacred symbols of Christian ministry, even the office itself, to speak a saving word on God's behalf.

The Grace of Daily Obligations:
Gail Godwin, *Evensong*

Born in Alabama and raised in Asheville, North Carolina, Gail Godwin's work is permeated by Southern sensibility even though she no longer resides in the South. Godwin's novels explore Southern themes such as family and land, the impingement of the past upon the present, caste and class, and the clash between conservative religious values and modern culture. She mines these concerns through careful attention to character, presenting the people in her stories with psychological realism.

In *Evensong*, Rev. Margaret Bonner is the Episcopal priest and rector of All Saints Church, in the Smoky Mountains resort village of High Balsam, North Carolina. As the thirty-three-year-old daughter of a deceased Episcopal priest, Rev. Bonner knows the ministry from the inside out.

One of the few women ministers to appear in Southern fiction, Bonner is portrayed sympathetically and realistically. Her internal thoughts are believable, as are the regular rounds of parish life: preparing sermons, presiding in worship, hearing confessions, visiting in the hospital, dealing with marriage and death. She refers to her life and work, partly in remembrance of her father, as the "grace of daily obligations."

She is smart, articulate, full of doubt and faith, and a sensitive priest who realizes her calling over time.[17]

We first encounter Margaret Bonner in Godwin's earlier novel *Father Melancholy's Daughter*. As with many clergy children, she struggles to understand her own vocation in the shadow of her father's. Margaret knows firsthand the depression of a clergy father who everyone calls "Father Melancholy" behind his back. Her father's depression begins when her mother, at twenty-eight years old, flees the clergy family because she cannot endure the confining role of southern Virginia Episcopal rector's wife. Her mother is a person whose "whole life had been spent among people who spoke in low-voiced, careful codes, the very cadences and word choices of their speech calculated to talk *around things*: to smoothe over, prettify, or exclude." Margaret bears the scars of these family wounds, which leave her with "dark, resentful moods as a motherless girl." Growing up, she had to be strong for her divorced father, a brilliant priest but troubled man.[18]

As Margaret clarifies her calling, she discusses her call to ministry with one of her seminary professors, Dr. Stroup, who is not convinced that Episcopal priesthood is a woman's vocation: "As you know, I haven't been an advocate of female priesthood. Doctrinally, I still can't reconcile myself to it." Margaret replies,

> My father had some of your reservations, Dr. Stroup, but I think if he were alive today, . . . I believe we'd be able to sit down together and work out our differences. . . . Don't you think we all store much of our knowledge on back shelves, until something . . . compels us to go back and reexamine it?

Gender matters in ministry. It is not enough for Margaret Bonner to sort out her own priestly vocation in relationship to that of her father. She must also contend with those like kindly Dr. Stroup who, though well intentioned, defend the ministry as a male, gentlemanly profession.[19]

Dr. Stroup represents the segments of the Episcopal Church (and other mainline Protestant denominations) that were opposed to the admission of women into ordained ministry when it was finally approved in 1976. To him, the arrival of women among the ordained destabilizes a sacred tradition that he feels compelled to defend. If Stroup can't keep women out of the ministry, he can do "everything in his power to disincline them from the appurtenances that would deface their office: lipstick, earrings, perfume, nail polish, jewelry, . . . anything that jiggled or jangled or distracted from what John Henry New-man had called 'the sacred dance of the ministers.' In other words, women may become ministers, but they should learn to act (and look) like men.[20]

Margaret sees Stroup's attitude and those who share it as a challenge but not a final impediment to fulfilling her call. These sorts of objections are predictable within a vocation that was for centuries an exclusively male privilege. On her way to becoming an Episcopal priest, Margaret Bonner must learn not only to listen to God but also to speak artfully to those who would close the doors of ministry upon her because she is a woman.[21]

Godwin does not grind an ideological ax regarding women in ministry. Bonner is not a political symbol of women's "rights" in the church. Rather, she is a competent priest who carries out her day-to-day responsibilities within church and community like so many female ministers in the South: with skill and grace.

Margaret Bonner is most clearly a priest when presiding at the liturgy of All Saints Episcopal Church. A love and respect for the poetry and theological integrity of the liturgy saturates Bonner's awareness. She is, for instance, particularly fond of the early (8:00 a.m.) Sunday service in the winter, and her love for it rings true for any minister or layperson who has communed with God and others in the simplicity of a quiet Sunday morning.

> I loved the winter eight o'clocks at All Saints High Balsam best. . . . Just a few determined souls setting forth in the first light to go and sit on wooden pews in an old brick building with a timber-trussed ceiling and a few special objects that focused their attention on something timeless they were drawn to, whether they understood it or not. No music or hymns or bells at this service, just the two altar candles lit and the readings for the day, a psalm said in unison. . . . Followed by Communion at the rail, exchanged greetings at the door (the only social contact of the day for some of them) and then home once more through the cold.

These are the people, and weekly worship is the time and place, that Rev. Bonner has been ordained to serve. Through the liturgy the priest points toward an ordered yet mysterious world overseen by "something timeless." At the center of that world is a table where the priest serves as host for the great Thanksgiving where believers celebrate "eternal companionship" in the sharing of bread and wine. Bonner's faithfulness to the liturgical tradition works in her favor. It leads to a "creative marriage" between the priest and the congregation.[22]

But despite her love of sacred ritual, Bonner does not cloister herself in the sanctuary. Her respect for the beauty of the liturgy is balanced by a realistic view of the grim side of existence. In fact, precisely because Bonner values Christian ritual and symbol, she is able to see deeply into the stinking crevasses of life. A faith whose primary initiation rite centers on the drowning of the self should quicken the pulse of the true believer. A communion liturgy that weekly reenacts the brutal slaughter of an innocent man is not a liturgy for the faint of heart. For example, reflecting on her clinical pastoral education experience in a metropolitan hospital in New York City, Bonner asks,

> Where is God in all of this? . . . Twenty-five beds filled with rape, shooting, and dope victims, and here's this young woman of eighteen, born to be beautiful, with oozing, fresh razor scars all over her face *and* sickle-cell anemia. . . . I never could look directly at this young woman's slashed-up beauty without fighting down the urge to run out of that ward and forsake my presumptuous dreams of improving the world.

Only a ritual that starts in death and ends in resurrection is sturdy enough to carry believers all the way through the suffering that humans inflict upon one another. Along the way, the suffering and the rituals will sometimes, by the grace of God, transform us into a more compassionate and forgiving people—at least that is the basic grammar of the faith that Rev. Margaret Bonner tries to learn and teach among the congregation.[23]

On another occasion she ministers to a troubled teenager, Josie, whose only meaningful relationships are imaginary ones with television characters. Abandoned by her parents, the youngster has no adult anchors to stabilize her through the turbulence of adolescence. Bonner enters the storm, offers the teenager an authentic relationship, and helps her to name her own feelings by reading the Psalms. Bonner also reaches out to Shaun, a young adult homosexual who is dying of AIDS. She helps him to put his final affairs in order and facilitates a death with dignity, blessing Shaun with oil before their final good-bye.

These weighty acts of ministry give the novel and its priest a theological and psychological depth. Bonner must be willing to enter into the ugly regions of human depravity, where as God's representative she wrestles with the hidden forces of sin, the "powers" and "principalities" that maim the human spirit and wreck the social order. As Bonner says about herself, "By nature I wasn't a pragmatist; I was a digger, a delver into complexities."[24]

Bonner's priesthood flows into a sensitive pastoral ministry. When, for example, she goes to the local hospital to care for a bereaved widow, Mrs. Britt, whose husband has just died, she invites the widow to call her by her first name, injecting a small but helpful note of humor into the grim moment.

> Most of them call me Pastor Margaret. It's a form just coming into use in our church that we all feel comfortable with. Though one old lady who didn't like me at first made a point of calling me "Mother" for a while. One time a little boy who was visiting called me Father— because of the vestments, I guess. But I wish you'd call me Margaret.

Mrs. Britt leans upon Margaret as she goes through the first hours of grief, helping the always proper elderly woman begin to voice her confusion and pain. "With Paul's health as uncertain as it was, I had ample opportunity to think about what it would be like without him. . . . But you never do get things quite right when you're preparing for them ahead of time." Or again, as she looks back on the final prayers read while her husband was dying, "While we were reading those beautiful words I've always found so moving at funerals, I thought, this is absurd, I don't believe a word of it, and Paul's no longer around to shield me from absurdity." Bonner hears such confidences without offering religious platitudes in the face of raw grief. When the time is right, however, and when asked by Mrs. Britt, "Where is God for you?" Bonner is able to gently reply with pastoral insight about the incarnation of God. "God," she says, is "definitely in the car with us as we talk and exchange things, and change each other in the process. . . . We need one another for God to work through us: that's something I experience every day." Although this incarnational view of God will not rescue Mrs. Britt from her loss, Bonner affirms that Mrs. Britt is not alone. Even more, Margaret communicates to Mrs. Britt that she still has something to give despite the death of her husband. Comfort and hope is all that Bonner has to offer. For those who are lost in grief, it is enough.[25]

Evensong concludes, appropriately, with Bonner presiding over a worship service. A fire has destroyed the congregation's beloved sanctuary, and the members gather among the ruins for Sunday worship.

Knowing the pastoral significance of the moment, the priest names the feelings that the loss of the building has provoked. "Each of us standing here cherishes some personal memory of something we will especially miss, a beautiful object that conveyed meaning, a particular place where we felt directly in the line of God's sight." She encourages the parishioners to mourn these losses by reading Psalm 102. But then she calls them to theological reflection upon the meaning of the church.

> We loved our building, yet we know that the church is us. The church is what we make when we come together in the sacramental mystery of God incarnate. . . . As people of God, what we need to be asking ourselves this morning is, what has God been doing here? What has God set in motion—through these circumstances—that we can carry forward and make more of?

Here is the priest as pastor. As priest, she trusts the liturgical tradition to speak to the current situation. As pastor, she sustains the congregation in the present loss while helping them to discern spiritual meaning for the future. No wonder some members call Rev. Bonner "Mother," others say "Pastor," and some just call her "Margaret."[26]

Margaret Bonner invites us to think intentionally about women in ministry, especially in the South. She helps us imagine a ministry—for women and men—that is spiritually wise and emotionally mature enough to act creatively and to take adversity in stride. But the fact remains that as a female minister, Rev. Bonner has many more hurdles to clear on her way to gaining congregational and cultural acceptance than do her male counterparts.[27]

For years the female minister has been waiting to be discovered by Southern writers. Changing social roles of women and men have permanently altered the landscape of North American society. Nevertheless, Southern fiction writers have been slow to pick up on this cultural and religious shift. Godwin's *Evensong* stands almost alone in Southern fiction for its portrayal of an ordained *female* minister.[28]

Even more remarkable, then, that Gail Godwin has given us a fresh image of the woman as priest in the South. Through Bonner, Godwin gives a clear-eyed assessment of the unique challenges of women in ministry as we move into the twenty-first century. Perhaps above all else, it is finally the authenticity of the call to ministry that will sustain clergywomen as they move forward. As Margaret Bonner says, "I wanted to do this more than anything else, . . . because it will always be too big for me and I can count on it to keep surprising me. Something in me craves the mystery of the adventure, I suppose."[29]

Ministry in the Ruins

Tennessean Peter Taylor offers another sober appraisal of the contemporary church and its ministers in the short story "The Decline and Fall of the Episcopal Church," which centers upon an elderly laymen's response to the slow deterioration and deconsecration of his beloved Episcopal chapel in rural West Tennessee. Thematically, it is reminiscent of both Walker Percy's concern for the collapse of Christian belief in the Western world and of Gail Godwin's exploration of religious tradition and change. Commenting on Rev. Flemming, the new Episcopal minister, the layman Thurston Rountree says, "But the new Episcopalians are different from the old sort that used to be there. One feels that they are all converts from other denominations. One feels this even about the Episcopal rector himself, nowadays." Flemming enrages Rountree when he says that the new church has to be established without any "relic from the past."[30]

On the surface Mr. Rountree sounds like one more High Church curmudgeon grousing about social and religious change. He's the kind of parishioner that will be a burr under the saddle of every priest who rides into town. But underneath, Rountree's observations strike the bedrock of ministry. As we have seen in Father John and Rev. Margaret Bonner, one of the greatest challenges for the contemporary priest is upholding church tradition while innovating with integrity. In trying to be relevant, the priest always runs the risk of losing his historical and ordained identity as a representative of Christ and the church.

From these priests in fiction, we learn anew of people's spiritual needs for constancy and tradition, as well as their genuine desire to be stimulated intellectually. Otherwise, religion declines and falls just like the old chapel in Peter Taylor's story or like the social structures that collapse around the characters in Walker Percy's novels. Ministers as priests are bearers of a sacred tradition. The thoughtful layperson knows that the sacred does not solely reside in a sanctuary or a baptismal fount, but the thoughtful believer also knows that the minister as priest bears primary responsibility for upholding the tradition.

It may well be, as some state, that the Christian church, including the juiced-up evangelical church of the South, is slowly imploding from the weight of its own complacency and pretense. Madness, like that of Lancelot Lamar, rushes howling among the ruins. But it may also be that as long as a few priests like Father John and Rev. Bonner know how to gather a faith-seeking people around a table set with bread and wine right among the ruins and utter the words, "Lift up your hearts," Christ-born hope remains.

6

Lying and Conniving and Claiming It as Heaven-Sent

The Minister as Con Man, Seducer, and Thief

God don't eat okra. . . . Youse livin' dirty and Ahm goin' tuh tell you 'bout it. Me and mah chillum got some rights. Big talk ain't changin' whut you doin'. You can't clean yo'self wid yo' tongue lak uh cat.
—Lucy Potts in Zora Neale Hurston's *Jonah's Gourd Vine*

The trick, Joel came to realize, was how to differentiate between heaven-sent persuasion and his own wish list, how to separate holy marching orders from the vanities and narcissistic wants that cluttered his brain.
—Rev. Joel King in Martin Clark's *Plain Heathen Mischief*

Beginning with the old Southwest humorists, Southern writers have zeroed in on the sins and shenanigans of the minister. Some write broadly, in the tradition of Mark Twain, to expose religious chicanery, to drag the miscreant minister out of the hayloft where he has been caught enjoying forbidden fruit, and to laugh as he runs through the field while picking buckshot out of his bare backside. Today's high-profile sexcapades of the Revs. Jimmy Swaggart and Jim Bakker remind us of these stories; except for the fact that they really happened, these cases seem to be parodies of parody, as if Swaggart and Bakker stepped right out of an Erskine Caldwell novel to imitate themselves. Other Southern writers, like Tennessee Williams (*Night of the Iguana*), plumb the tormented spirits of whiskey priests and sift basic questions of Christian doctrine: Is the sacrament received from the hands of a drunken minister still a sacrament? Still other writers, such as James Baldwin (*Go Tell It on the Mountain*) and William Faulkner (*As I Lay Dying*), dramatize a minister's infidelity and then show the destructive consequences of his adulterous behavior. Especially in the arenas of sex and money, writers regularly tell about ministers misbehaving.

Southern writers, in particular, have long cast their lines in ponds well stocked with bottom-feeding ministers. The money-grubbing and sexually leeching ministers that writers pull thrashing out of Southern religious waters put flesh upon H. L. Mencken's caustic observation about the South and religion: the "bunghole of the United States, a cesspool of Baptists, a miasma of Methodism, snake-charmers, phony real-estate operators, and syphilitic evangelists."[1]

The issue is clergy character. How do the actions of the minister and his whole personhood align with professed beliefs and the moral norms of the community? As Richard Lischer says, "In the last analysis, the pastoral *character* humbly offers itself as a paradigm for the service, worship, and witness to God that belongs to all believers. It's not better performances the church needs, but truer characters." It is simply not enough when the ordained minister stumbles to claim that he "has needs" like every other sinner. Of course the minister has "needs"; he's a human being and a sinner like everyone else. The difference is this: as ordained representative of the peculiar people called Christians, like it or not, the minister lives as a public person. She is an official symbol bearer for the community that lives under the sign of the cross. When she stumbles under the weight of her own fallen humanity, the community also staggers as it tries to bear her up with the grace of Christ. Tragically, sometimes the church must locate another emblem bearer.[2]

The sins of the ordained minister are publicly magnified. Clergy immorality unleashes shock waves through a congregation, as anyone knows who has passed through a church trauma resulting from financial embezzlement or sexual abuse by the minister. Only the healthiest congregations emerge from ministerial scandal without debilitating wounds, and then only by the grace of God. Scars remain. Jesus' admonition regarding harm to others comes to mind. "It would be better for you if a great millstone were fastened around your neck and you were drowned in the depth of the sea" (Matthew 18:6). As Gregory the Great said, "No one does more harm in the church than he, who having the title or rank or holiness, acts evilly." It seems burdensome to ministers, but as an ordained representative of the church, ministerial character always matters.[3]

Southern writers do not indulge clergy misconduct. They reserve their sharpest barbs for the errant minister—precisely because so much is at stake. As cultural watchdogs, writers call the ministry and the church to account, no matter how much they may overdraw their characters. They call for vigilance against the religious shysters who con their way through Southern churches and, when exposed, slink off to fleece other naive congregations.

The underbelly of straitlaced Southern religiosity comes out not only in the immorality of the ministers but also in the congregations of the South. The misbehaving minister *and* the congregation are both easy targets for satire when the minister tries to get away with tomfoolery before the scrutinizing public, especially in small towns of the South where "preacher watching" is a regular pastime. As people, we generally take perverse pleasure from exposing in others the very same sins that we keep hidden within ourselves. If we can spot someone else playing hanky-panky, especially if it's the minister, then we can feel better about our own dirty secrets, real or imagined.

In some instances, the minister and the congregation are locked into a mutually reinforcing hypocrisy. The preacher may be the lead villain, but he is supported by a cast of congregational characters who perversely indulge in their own undoing. It's hard to know who to hold most at fault: the plundering minister or the congregation who trusts him to take all the money to the bank.

The minister is a complex character. Both human beings and resident holy persons, ministers act out their struggles with faith and doubt upon the public stage of church and community. The public scrutinizes almost every facet of their lives. From professional obligations to family relations, the minister is always on display. No matter how grounded in God and secure in self, the shadow of sin falls upon the minister just as upon every other human being. When the sin of the minister becomes magnified by communal scrutiny, precisely because the community expects the parson (the public person) to bear the standard of morality for themselves, the minister appears to be the chief among all sinners.

God Don't Eat Okra: The Excuses and Abuses of the Natural Man in Zora Neale Hurston's *Jonah's Gourd Vine*

Reverend John Pearson, Baptist preacher and "a natchel man," is the principal character of Zora Neale Hurston's first novel, *Jonah's Gourd Vine*, originally published in 1934, three years before Hurston's more highly acclaimed *Their Eyes Were Watching God*. Set in southern Alabama and northern Florida around the African American town of Eatonville, where Hurston grew up, *Jonah's Gourd Vine* displays Hurston's keen ear for the dialogue of early-twentieth-century rural Southern blacks (down to phonetically reproducing black speech), the folkways of the African American people of the old South, race relations within a changing South, and most significantly, the place of religion within the African American culture during the early twentieth century.

John Pearson comes of age as a young man accustomed to hard work within a family of black tenant farmers in the Jim Crow South. Vestiges of the Old South plantation system are still in place, including the inter-racial sexual relationship between John's African American mother, Amy Crittenden, and Alf Pearson, the white landowner, which results in John's conception. Pearson's wealthy white landowner father demonstrates paternal affection, and his strong and loving mother dotes on her firstborn. He marries the winsome Lucy Potts, a member of Macedonia Baptist Church, who first notices his way with words. Along with the church deacons, Lucy encourages his interest in the ministry. "Dat boy is called tuh preach and don't know it. Ahm gwine tell him so."[4]

With such encouragement, Pearson claims for himself that "God done called me tuh preach" and begins a lifelong ministry among the Baptists of northern Florida. The church folk draw out his natural gift for language. "Ah knowed it! Tole 'im long time uhgo dat's what he wuz cut out fuh. Thang God." Commenting to Lucy about his way with words, Pearson says, "Lucy, look lak Ah jus' found out whut Ah kin do. De words dat sets de church on fire comes tuh me jus' so. Ah reckon de angels must tell 'em tuh me." His preaching "scatters fire" among the congregation. His rhythmic sermons draw from the rich treasury of Scripture, nature, and the proverbs of his African ancestors.[5]

But a worm eats away at this Jonah's gourd vine of a man. Like the biblical namesake of the book's title, Pearson has a divine calling. But he rebels against God at every turn. Pearson's self-centeredness first shows up in his relationship with his long-suffering wife, Lucy. Pearson is an unsurpassed preacher, but he is also a self-proclaimed "natchel man" whose desire for other women Lucy cannot break. Though he professes undying love for Lucy, he sullies their covenant through affairs with other women both inside and outside of the church. When Lucy confronts Pearson, he defends himself by saying, "Dat's de brute-beast in me" and "Don't tell me 'bout dem trashy women Ah lusts after once in uh while. Dey's less dan leaves uh grass. Lucy do you still love me lak yuh useter?" Lucy, ready to forgive, replies, "Yeah John, and mo'. Ah got mo' tuh love yuh fuh now."[6]

Therein lies the canker at the heart of their marriage. Pearson, like an alcoholic to drink, continues to sneak around with other women while Lucy forgives and even defends him. Though he humiliates her, Lucy helps Pearson avoid the consequences of his behavior within the congregation.

Nevertheless, there are limits to Lucy's tolerance. A feisty woman who wants to preserve their marriage, she challenges Pearson by saying that no matter how slick he is, God can still grease him. "God don't eat okra," she chides. She rebukes Pearson by saying that all the fancy preaching in the world will not wash away his sinfulness. "You can't clean yo'self wid you' tongue lak uh cat." Lucy threatens to leave Pearson if he doesn't stop his carousing. He answers Lucy's threat with a violent warning: "If you ever start out de door tuh leave me, you'll never make it tuh de gate. Ah means tuh blow yo' heart out and hang fuh it."[7]

The worm that gnaws away at Pearson is not only self-centeredness that leads to adultery but also violence that leads to abuse. As he smacks Lucy in the face, he commands, "Ah tole yuh tu hush"; then he goes outside to stand among the palmetto bushes "feeling like a Nebuchadnezzar in his exile." Once the violence begins, it escalates as the minister tries to beat the cause of his own shame out of his wife. Lucy becomes increasingly ill and withdrawn, attended to by her sympathetic daughter, Isis, and a caring church member, Sister Clarke. As Lucy sinks in despair toward death, she says to Sister Clarke, "Ah done been in sorrow's kitchen and Ah done licked out all de pots. Ah done died in grief and been buried in de bitter waters, and Ah done rose agin from de dead lak Lazarus."[8]

Lucy's slow death chastens but finally does not change Pearson. He fears her death and rebuke. But when she dies, Pearson is perversely exultant. He is free of the guilt provoked by Lucy's knowledge of his adultery and violence. "There was no more sin. Just a free man having his will of women. He was glad in his sadness." On the surface, Rev. Pearson appears to mourn the loss of "sweet Lucy," but underneath he anticipates how his newfound freedom will allow him to exploit other women.[9]

After Lucy's death, Rev. Pearson continues to abuse and take advantage of other women. He marries his consort, Hattie Tyson, but he soon begins to attack and blame her for his own failings. Power and powerlessness fuel Pearson's domestic abuse. He is a talented though insecure minister who physically violates women to compensate for his own weaknesses. In the twisted logic of the abuser, violence perpetrated upon others becomes the sacrament that leads to repentance and reconciliation. Never mind that Pearson pummels his victims into submission. The abuser is never concerned about the emotional, spiritual, or physical well-being of his victims, only his own need to dominate and control.[10]

The startling thing is the complicity of the congregation. Pearson's promiscuity and violence take place within a community and a congregation that is ambivalent about his behavior. While the wisest members of the congregation know that his actions are sinful, they withhold moral censure because he is the anointed one of God. They judge the female victims while excusing the male minister's abuse. Even as Pearson ages and loses some of his preaching ability, many members continue to support him. "He had still enough of the former John to be formidable as an animal and enough of his Pagan poesy to thrill."[11]

Tragically, what the congregation overlooks by their support of this graying yet still roaming lion is the suffering of his victims. No matter how sincere Pearson's struggle with his own natural "urges," and no matter how widespread the practice of clergy philandering in Hurston's day or our own, the fact remains that the ordained minister's misuse of authority brings torment upon others. Pearson's first wife, Lucy, dies because of his emotional and physical abuse. He nearly beats to death his second wife, Hattie, who then must endure a humiliating public trial to get restitution. At the end of the novel, Pearson seems to reform, only to later relapse and take sexual advantage of Ora, an impoverished young woman. When Pearson rationalizes his actions, it only underscores how he objectifies these women. He considers them to be either temptresses who lure him into sexual liason or nags who deserve his violence. That some within the congregation defend Pearson shows just how far the church will go to cover up for its leaders.

All of this violation finally bears down upon the guilty Pearson when his car crashes into a train (the train of judgment). His funeral is fitting. For one who has caused so much suffering for others, there is no final celebration. There is no "drum of triumph, that speaks of great ancestors." No "drum of kidskin, for that is to dance with joy and to call to mind birth and creation." For John Pearson, this talented but tormenting minister of the gospel, there is only "the voice of Death—that promises nothing, that speaks with tears only, and of the past." Pearson does not go to the grave as the celebrated preacher whom many admired. His character pronounces the final sentence. The best the presiding minister can say at John Pearson's funeral is, "He wuz uh man, and nobody knowed 'im but God."[12]

The destructive dynamics of this clergy story exist today every bit as much as in the 1930s of Hurston's novel. A recent, high-profile case in Tennessee involved a minister's wife who shot and killed her husband after enduring years of "silent abuse." Within the congregation, he was the model pastor and she, the supportive wife. But in the privacy of their home, the clergy husband dominated and abused. Emotionally and physically depleted, the wife struck back and killed her husband. This is only one of many such tragedies that occur across the United States every year. In Protestant and Catholic circles alike, sexual abuse happens with alarming frequency, and both branches of the church waiver in their commitment to deal forthrightly with these violations.[13]

The primary issue of clergy sexual abuse is misuse of power and authority. Pearson's crime is not that he is a "natural man," a sinner like all the rest, but that he chooses not to recognize how his sexual domination of women destroys their relationship with God. The violation is particularly egregious because of the sacred trust that binds the minister-parishioner relationship. The minister who wanders or willingly crosses the physical and emotional boundaries that necessarily exist between minister and parishioner drags the other person into a land that is haunted by the absence of God and stained with self-recrimination. When the parishioner awakens to the horror that she or he has been abused by a minister of the gospel, many find it difficult to believe in God or participate in the church ever again. The violating minister, on the other hand, is more interested in covering up his mistakes or finding another prey than in the spiritual and emotional health of his previous victims. He may feign concern for the women, men, or children that he has violated, and even go through bouts of agonizing guilt as did John Pearson, but unless the church permanently stops him, which should always mean removal of ordination, he will eventually violate again. It takes a strong woman, such as Hurston's Lucy Potts, to come through the violence and philandering of her husband and be able to defiantly say, "Ah done been in sorrow's kitchen and Ah done licked out all de pots."[14]

Does this mean that the church should never forgive abusive ministers? No, the church that lives by the redemptive grace of Christ always forgives, even its sinful ministers who damage the body of Christ. But forgiveness does not entail restoration of ordained status. The church has every right to expect its ministers to conform their personal and social ethics to the character of Christ, in whose name they preach and serve the sacraments. When the minister violates the sacred trust of the congregation, then the church rightfully asks the ordained minister to surrender his ordination and return to the pews. As William Willimon notes, "We are not being naively idealistic or demandingly unrealistic when we ask our leaders to be exemplary persons and, when they show that they are not, to ask them to remove themselves from positions of leadership." Theologically speaking, he is still in the same relationship with God that he was before and during ordination—a sinner yet redeemed—but functionally speaking, he is no longer the right person to officially represent the ministry of all believers.[15]

What does this say about the doctrine of ex opere operato ("from the work done"), the understanding that the effectiveness of the sacraments does not depend upon the moral character of the minister? Does the efficacy of preaching, since many would argue that preaching is a Protestant sacrament, depend upon the moral character of the minister? By his sexual immorality, does Pearson negate the power of his preaching? No. The preacher like all Christians holds the treasures of faith in "earthen vessels." God can and does choose to act through sermons and sacraments delivered by tainted hands. As any quick study of Scripture reveals, God can bring reconciliation through rascally leaders, from Jacob to David, from Peter to Paul. But the representative nature of the ordained ministry requires a Christian whose character is marked by virtues such as compassion, temperance, justice, and fortitude. This is so because the minister stands between the congregation and God, representing God to the people and the people to God. Augustine, to whom we can trace the doctrine of ex opere operato in his controversy with the Donatists, marks this tension when he says in a sermon, "For you I am a bishop, but with you I am a Christian." It may sound harsh, but the character of some ministers is so flawed that with them in the way, the congregation can hardly see themselves or God. As Willimon puts it, "The congregation is quite right in expecting that we are at least attempting, to a greater or lesser degree, to embody the faith that we proclaim." Some ministers are so unaware of the harm that they are doing to themselves and those in their care that they should be relieved of their ordained authority.[16]

Most ministers are not as dismissive of ministerial ethics as John Pearson. Ministers are complex characters painted in shades of gray. Among ministers, the sensational sins of the flesh or of theft usually begin with the quieter and more insidious sins of boredom (acedia), ignoring of Sabbath, failure to cultivate friendships, neglect of one's own family, or trying to please everyone. Such garden-variety sin can ultimately land the minister in a heap of trouble, even though the beginning of character deterioration is almost imperceptible. Ministers in the South and everywhere else should pay as much attention to where ethical decline begins as to where it leads. Such is the case of Rev. Joel King in Martin Clark's *Plain Heathen Mischief*.[17]

Lying, Cheating, and Stealing to Arrive at the Ultimate Good: Martin Clark, *Plain Heathen Mischief*

Martin Clark, resident of Stuart, Virginia, sets *Plain Heathen Mischief* in contemporary Roanoke, Virginia, and Missoula, Montana. The novel is part character study of Rev. Joel King, part mystery, and part legal thriller. In Joel King we see a minister who tries to justify lying, cheating, and stealing to arrive at a better good.

Rev. Joel King is the forty-two-year-old pastor of the establishment Roanoke First Baptist Church. A graduate of Southeastern Seminary at Wake Forest, North Carolina, King is successfully ensconced in the ministry. He is a serious-minded pastor and husband, well liked by the congregation.

> While he hadn't been bold with his theology or a barn burner in the pulpit, he had been a steadfast pillar for his church, a tall, strapping, honest man whose acts were full of diligence . . . and whose thoughtful sermons went directly to the point. He had won his congregation's trust and affections because of his rapturous dedication to even the most distasteful aspects of his duties.[18]

Tension in the story begins when King wanders across the physical boundaries with a worldly-wise, spoiled seventeen-year-old parishioner Christy Darden. Though Christy entraps the minister in order to levy a lawsuit against the church, King knows that he bears the responsibility for this sin: "He'd violated whatever religious impulse she ever had and done little or nothing to expand it." For King, it does not matter that he and Christy never actually have intercourse. He has succumbed to temptation, wandered into "plain heathen mischief." A Bible-believing Baptist, the minister knows that he should not avoid the consequences of his sin, which include the loss of his ministry, the breakdown of his marriage, and a criminal record that cannot be expunged. Willing to take his punishment, King resigns from the church and accepts the six-month prison sentence for "corruption of a minor."[19]

When released from prison, King carries an unpaid burden of guilt that he desperately wants to rectify. Pained by his offense to God, his wife, to Christy, and to his church members, the defrocked minister decides to take matters into his own hands, or to put it theologically, to earn his own salvation. He wants to financially repay everyone for his mistakes, including his supportive sister, Sophie. So he becomes involved in a high-priced insurance scam with shady lawyers and pawnbrokers that includes a jewelry theft and a double-cross of his criminal associates. As he rationalizes to Sophie, "I get tons of money to give to you and the church. I'm only going to keep enough to pay the court costs. The rest is for you, and Baker [her son] and Roanoke First Baptist."[20]

The strategy cannot succeed. Sophie does not hesitate to tell him why when he divulges his plan to swindle his partners in crime.

> It seems to me you've managed to leap into the cesspool and become as corrupt and dishonest as your friends. . . . You lied. Lied under oath as I understand it. And you are stealing from the company that has to pay this bogus claim, ripping off people for a lot of money. You think everything is washed clean because you plan to donate the money to a church and your pitiful, ragtag sister?

Sophie becomes livid when King rationalizes that he has to rectify things. "The Lord wants us to carry a little of our own load," he says. She counters, "Yeah and to carry it honestly, Joel. . . . You've conned yourself if you truly believe half the bullshit you're saying, and that's tragic." Like Sisyphus, King keeps trying to push the boulder of his moral failure uphill, and it continues to crash down upon him.[21]

Sophie reminds her brother that as an ordained minister he has failed to heed his own message. "You're supposed to be the preacher, not me," she says in exasperation. "Seems the question is how deep your faith runs, and yours is fairly shallow. . . . I'm not as sold on religion as you are—far from it—but I do believe in decency and a few absolutes." Joel defends himself against Sophie's piercing honesty: "I'm trying to do the right thing, to fix my error and serve the Lord." But Sophie will not be manipulated by King's piety. She is the kind of sister who could keep any minister humble. She bores in on King's presumptuousness about God's support of his efforts.

> And I'm sure He's mighty proud of your efforts. Delighted. It was especially good of Him to suspend all the normal rules for you and still let you use His name while you were setting affairs in order here on earth. Doing *His* will, right? Lying and conniving and stealing to promote God's agenda. Yessir, I'm sure the banquet table is arranged and the goblets are ready with wine—you've done well, carried the banner high.

With this tongue-lashing from the morally decent Sophie, King is one step closer to coming clean, to surrendering the pride that drives a wedge between him and God.[22]

From here on out, King undergoes a rapid series of encounters that contribute to his moral education and restoration. For example, he meets another minister in whose flaws King is able to see himself. He realizes that "he and the poor fellow and everyone else were alike, clay and dust, forever imperfect, hamstrung by the Fall and a snake's beguiling charm but still precious in the Lord's eyes." He confesses his white-collar crime to the local district attorney, who shows him no pity—"You lie a lot for a man of the cloth"—but who treats him with fairness and respect. He finds employment at a local fly-fishing shop, whose decent and honest owner, Dixon Kreager, becomes a friend, and who vouches for him with the district attorney that King is "a good man." Kreager weighs King "by his own set of standards" and does not find him wanting.[23]

These gifts of human decency affect King. These people do not support him because he is their pastor but because he is a good human being who wants but can't seem to figure out how to do the right thing. As Sophie says, "There's goodness in you; you just haven't been in the everyday world long enough to know how to set it loose." Every minister should tape this understanding of character to the bathroom mirror: virtue does not come through grand gestures of altruism or self-humiliation but through daily acts of kindness and compassion guided by principle. Unlike Joel, his supporters do not presume to know what God wants or how God will act within human creation.

King slides into moral corruption because, as a basically good person, he tries to expiate his guilt by making things right for others. The more he schemes and lies, the deeper the ditch he digs between himself and God. King is compelling because he is a good man who makes disastrous choices and then tries to justify them on religious grounds. Unlike Zora Neale Hurston's John Pearson, whose flaws are extreme from start to finish, Joel King descends by degrees. He searches for how to make things right with God and those whom he loves, but he chooses an immoral path to accomplish his goals. For King, the ends justify the means. It's OK to set up a fake jewelry heist and scam the insurance company for the payout if he intends to use the illegal settlement to repay those whom he has wronged. As he says to Sophie when she challenges his actions, "I bent the rules for the greater good, to do justice."

Trying to understand his actions, King says, "It all just crept up on me piecemeal, and before I know it I'm in a quagmire and there's no escaping. But I'm still not sure where the train jumped the tracks."[24]

This is an authentic depiction of a minister tangled in the spiderweb of self-chosen sin and looking for a way out. Some would argue that King is "drawn" into corruption by the teenager, Christy. All other deceits grow out of his response to this enticement. But Joel King has too much integrity for that. As he says, "There's no such creature as a minor sin. I believe that, and I deserved punishment." His unethical behavior worsens as he tries to correct his mistakes. As he says to Sophie, "I was at least trying to do the Lord's mission, was aware of right and wrong and the big picture. Maybe my tack was misguided, but I've always meant to arrive at the ultimate good. I wanted to repay the church as best I could." Wanting to wrest good from bad, he plunges ahead into further deception.[25]

King finally recognizes in good Calvinist fashion that he is simply not in control of his own life or that of anyone else. He cannot cheat, lie, or connive to promote God's agenda; he cannot prove his own goodness after falling into sin. "I thought I was in charge and doing big things, tried to put the Lord on terms. What an idiot." Behind all that has happened, Joel recognizes the inscrutable design of God. "I've been so far behind the curve it's pathetic. . . . My attempts to deliver punishment and fine-tune justice were about as significant as the doodles of a preschooler or the downstroke of a gnat's wing."[26]

These are the words of a forgiven man. After all his self-justifying shenanigans, King finally comes to the place of surrender. No longer must he shoulder the burden of his own redemption. Even though he must return to prison for his self-serving crimes, Joel believes that he is "a rich man, wealthy in the sense [he] always desired to be."[27]

You would think that a Baptist preacher would know the meaning of grace, but it takes Rev. King forty-two years to discover it for himself. He falls, but he falls "toward grace" and goes off to prison, calm and serene, assured now that God is in control. He becomes, Sophie realizes, "a man formed and reformed . . . his deliverance was obvious and undeniable even in the transient light, and she was at that instant convinced, believed in the truth of his contentment and that his coffers were full of the coin he most desired."[28]

It takes Rev. Joel King half a lifetime to become an ordinary Christian. Along the way, he harms others, especially Christy, his congregation, and his wife, and he brings shame upon himself. Many ministers find themselves walking this same destructive path. Through the twists and turns of ministry, one deception leads to the next. Wanting to live by grace, we instead seek to justify our every action. Ensnared by our own sin, we thrash around in an attempt to put things right, only to create a bigger mess for ourselves and others.

But in the end, Joel King's is a hopeful story. For he is a fallen minister finally awakened to the riches of God's grace. He has gone through the refiner's fire and emerged as a more humble, honest Christian. Maybe, upon his release from prison, he will be able to more truly minister to others. As he concludes, "I've got a story to tell, and I've earned my stripes. I believe I could bring something to the table." What he brings to the table is a clearer understanding of his own humanity and his own need for grace and forgiveness. Such recognition will translate into a more grace-filled ministry with others. Ordained or not, Joel King the reformed sinner will be able to honestly share with others what it is to be a sinner saved by grace.[29]

The Hope of Sin

These two ministers, John Pearson and Joel King, suggest the paradoxical hope lodged within human sin. In our acknowledged sinfulness, we discover an opening to God. As Thomas Merton puts it, "In the end, it comes down to the old story that we are sinners, but that this is our hope because sinners are the ones who attract to themselves the infinite compassion of God." And as the apostle Paul expresses the same conviction, "Where sin increased, grace abounded all the more" (Romans 5:20).[30]

As unattractive as Pearson and King are, both wrestle with the most Southern of religious themes in literature: sin, guilt, and redemption. Pearson never comes to terms with his sinfulness; in the end, it destroys him. King faces the consequences of his sin and discovers redemption on the other side. Some unethical ministers may be able to erase their own moral conscience, such as John Pearson, but others, like Joel King, cannot. They are con men, abusers, and thieves, but they cannot outfox God. Even while fleecing the flock, they remain "Christ-haunted," whether they meet their Savior on the receiving end of a train wreck (John Pearson) or while fulfilling a prison sentence (Joel King).

These ministers remind us that sin has its price, especially for those whose offense is multiplied because it occurs within a congregation of believers. Even if congregations are slow to condemn, ministers who violate the sacred trust of their people do not escape a day of reckoning. Like David confronted by Nathan (2 Samuel 12), the sin of the minister will come to light either in self-condemnation or social castigation. Some fallen ministers, like Joel King, will emerge from the prison of sin purified, humbled, and more aware of the mystery of God. Others, more self-centered, like John Pearson, will continue to walk the rails of sin until the locomotive crushes them.

These wayward ministers cast light upon the moral ambiguity of the Christian ministry for all of us. Many ministers find themselves in situations similar to those of Joel King and John Pearson. Though only a human being, a sinner yet saved by grace, the minister is a *called* and *representative* human being, one who stands under orders from God within the Christian congregation. It is frightfully easy to abuse the authority of the office, whether by taking sexual advantage of one's parishioners or by lying, cheating, and stealing from them. Though violating ministerial ethics, it is easy enough for the deceiving clergy to hide behind the robe and collar.

The problem is spiritual and theological. When the minister forgets his dependence upon grace, sin storms the house. When he forgets who he represents, he defiles himself and others. Sordid and dull, of no value to the congregation and its story, they will rightfully set him aside.

But when the minister in humility and trust aligns himself with the grace of God given through Jesus Christ, he becomes a character worth watching, a sinner who knows the ways and means of redemption. Or as Rev. Joel King puts it, a minister who truly understands that he is a sinner yet saved by grace is a minister who has "something to bring to the table."[31]

7

A Good Church Slogan Is Hard to Come By

The Minister as Church Politician, Institutional Salesman, and Company Manager

Maybe no religion could survive the short journey from the wholesome filth of a stable . . . to the sterile sickness of spires and the grand ballrooms of McCormick Place on the Lake. Have we so muffled the little bitty baby's cry, the mother's wail that all hope is gone forever? Have we so amplified the steepled rhetoric of doctrine—doctrine without discipleship—that we can do nothing?
— Miriam in Will D. Campbell's *The Convention*

Had he not made the career-fatal mistake of marrying me, Ben Lynch would've been where he wanted to go, top of the ladder of the United Methodist Church. . . . To be a successful preacher, however, he needed a wife, and he needed one quick.
— Dean Lynch in Cassandra King's *The Sunday Wife*

Ministry falls apart without effective church administration. Clergy are ordained to the ministry of "word, sacrament, *and order*." Someone must organize the various ministries of the congregation, and this frequently is the responsibility of the ordained leader. Some ministers are skilled at blending the various gifts of the congregation into a healthy body of believers who serve God and neighbor. But danger lies in the possibility of the minister becoming captive to church politics, institutional salesmanship, and managerial endeavors. When the minister is owned by the culture and becomes, in theologian Carlyle Marney's words, "a successful blesser of a successful culture," this is a call to arms for Southern writers.[1]

Problems occur when an ordained leader *primarily* understands her role as company manager rather than as administrative servant and becomes wedded to business management models of leadership. Consumed by protecting the physical, social, and moral boundaries of the church, she fixates on bottom-line financial concerns or the enhancement and security of the church as a "corporation." The result is, as a parishioner says to the minister in Robert Morgan's *This Rock*, "You spend your

time keeping people out, rather than bringing them in." When it comes
to change, this minister is, at best, a gradualist and usually a defender of
the status quo. Most problematically, she mistakes the people of God for
a religious business and the church member as a paying customer.[2]

A far cry from the disciples of the New Testament who risk their lives
to follow an empire-threatening Christ, the minister as institutional
salesman aggressively works to extend the church's status within the culture. He is found in both conservative and liberal congregations. In the
former, he may espouse a thinly disguised doctrine of national patriot-
ism under the guise of "kingdom building." In other congregations, the
minister as institutional salesman presides over megachurches and
megabudgets whose worship and congregational life frequently mirror
the trends of consumer culture, from musical styles to latte machines in
the church lobby. All of it is designed to make the church attendee feel
comfortable and plugged in to God.

These ministers can be found in every denomination across the
South. They covet personal power and public praise and serve in support of a hierarchy that rewards loyalty with institutional success.
Service to the congregation and community becomes simply a means
to greater economic and political advancement up the denominational ladder. The real faces of the people recede as the minister manages a busy-all-the-time shop to increase market share and jostle for
political power. The actual tasks of ministry become burdensome
because their spiritual intent has been hollowed out by the minister's
self-preoccupation. Over time, the minister seeks to avoid those
whom God has entrusted to him.[3]

Two contemporary novels trade upon the image of the minister as
church politician, institutional salesman, and company manager: Will
Cambell's *The Convention* and Cassandra King's *The Sunday Wife*. Significantly, in both novels male ministers are portrayed negatively while
women push, sometimes forcefully, sometimes quietly, against the male,
hierarchical understandings of power and authority that motivate the men.

God Wants It Done Now: Cut by Stained Glass
in Will Campbell's *The Convention*

Will D. Campbell, preacher, pastor, storyteller, onetime civil rights
activist, provocateur, and thorn in the flesh of institutional Christianity, is a paradoxical figure in Southern religious and literary life. Native

of Amite County, Mississippi, and longtime resident of Mt. Juliet, Tennessee, he is a Southern evangelical Christian in touch with his rural roots who will not be bamboozled by ecclesiastical pretension of any stripe. An unapologetic iconoclast, Campbell steadfastly affirms his faith in Jesus Christ while also believing that the institutional church is "the single greatest barrier to the propagation of the gospel." This sentiment runs straight through his life and stories. Marshall Frady describes him as one of God's "divine fools." He dares to speak truth to power while celebrating the generosity of spirit, compassion, forgiveness, and courage of simple Christian faith.[4]

The Convention, published in 1988, is a thinly veiled send-up of the Southern Baptist Church's turn to fundamentalism in the 1980s. Though names have been changed and circumstances altered, the Federal Baptist Church (FBC) of the novel obviously parallels the Southern Baptist Convention (SBC). The principal minister, Dr. Roger Hagan, bears marked resemblance to two Texas ministers, Drs. W. A. Criswell and Paige Patterson, who helped orchestrate the overthrow of the denomination's moderate leadership. Campbell uncompromisinglty exposes the political machinations of Dr. Roger Hagan, who is up for election as president of the convention, and of former U.S. Senator Purdue, the power behind the throne. Both men unashamedly scheme to control every aspect of the denomination's doctrine and direction. They are especially keen to maintain their power by excluding women from ordination.

But they face an unexpected challenge from Dorcas McBride of Scotts Grove, Mississippi. A simple, yet devout Christian, McBride is the antithesis of the ecclesiastical wheeler-dealers who control the convention. A Bible-believing follower of Christ, she values the dignity of all persons, honest speech, the nurture of family and land, the *shared* authority of husbands and wives in church and home, compassion for the weak and the outsider, and freedom of personal belief. Dorcas is unexpectedly catapulted into the spotlight of the national convention when, at the urging of other female delegates, she runs for president, carrying with her the hopes of many women and disenfranchised members of the church. If successful, she will be the first elected female president of the Federal Baptist Convention, an event that Hagan and Purdue will do everything within their power to avert.

Campbell shows no sympathy for the likes of minister Roger Hagan. His hardball tactics and vicious attacks upon women and homosexuals would seem far-fetched were it not for the background that informs Campbell's story. Campbell lays bare the ambition, vanity, and fear (of loss of control) that motivates Doctor Hagan's politically charged ministry.

The ordained ministers in this novel worship at the altar of self rather than of God. As Miriam, one of the women who opposes Dr. Hagan, says, "They made an idol out of their movement and called it church." It is a toss-up as to which the reader might find most offensive—Dr. Hagan's narcissism or the conspicuous consumption that accompanies it. Swapping success stories with another minister (a Freudian game of "Who's got the biggest steeple?"), the preening Hagan sighs, "It's a humbling experience to know that two hundred buses haul people every Sunday to hear you preach." Then he and the other ministers and their wives discuss "which church provides which couple with the largest parsonage." Reflecting on the luxurious lifestyles of these Baptist preacher superstars who live in million-dollar homes maintained by the tithes of the faithful, Vernon Hedge, a displaced moderate member of the convention, laments, "We have always loved Jesus but we have never trusted Him."[5]

If the vanity and consumerism of these minister politicians is not unsavory enough, there is the unapologetic Christian empire building. Fearful that their movement is losing steam, Hagan and Senator Purdue hire a public relations firm to help them increase "market share" for the denomination. "A good slogan is hard to come by," declares Purdue. Their high-priced slogan, "A Million More in Ninety-Four," becomes the rallying cry for a calculated "mission outreach" in ethnic neighborhoods across the country. Roger Hagan's election banner on the convention floors says it all: A VOTE FOR ROGER HAGAN IS A VOTE FOR THE KINGDOM'S WORK.[6]

But what is really going on is an effort to control the country's political agenda. Will Campbell knows that when religious leaders bed down with partisan politicians, the scenario is troubling. The church leaders of Campbell's novel confuse their own wills with God's will and are ruthless in trying to establish their own religious and moral convictions as the law of the land. When their agenda is threatened, they will "fix" the problem by changing the rules that govern the convention, or call upon the president of the United States to shore up their platform, or even become violent with their opponents.

Campbell challenges a complacent church and public to remove the scales from their eyes. Ministers should take note: confusing one's own beliefs with the will of God, and then systematically institutionalizing those beliefs within a nation's laws and programs is a dangerous move toward totalitarianism, which thinking Christians must resist in the name of a liberating Christ. Campbell scratches out this word of caution as much for liberal Christian believers as for conservatives, for both sides are prone to mistake their own agenda for God's will. Social observer David Dark comments perceptively on the current entanglement of Christian fundamentalism and politics in America:

> Within an egocentric and vulnerable American culture, inspiring confidence (or faith in one's faith) is slowly unmasked as the Devil's primary weapon of mass destruction. The faith that is its own justification leads to the violence that believes itself to be liberation and righteousness and always in the service of virtue.[7]

The frightening truth is that the self-justification of the fundamentalist minister (whether Christian, Muslim, or Jewish) will not stop with denominational wars. Fundamentalists are more than willing to carry the flag of their brand of truth into national and international wars to stop violence by using violence in the name of a peace-loving God. The enemy is "out there" according to minister Hagan, and with enough political clout the church can crush the foe with the boot of Christ and make the world safe for democracy and Christianity. With a sardonic smile, Campbell shows in *The Convention* how one Christian denomination, based in the South, goes about wreaking unholy havoc.

It comes as little surprise that Hagan's authoritarian brand of evangelical Christianity conceals a violence toward women. The extreme authoritarian personalities of Roger Hagan and his followers cannot tolerate dissent, especially from women, and so, as the women of the convention begin to gain steam for their presidential candidate, Dorcas McBride, Hagan and Purdue crack down. Hagan says, "It may be their right to run a woman, but whoever this Dorcas Rose is, she doesn't believe in the Bible. God's Word sure as sin says that women can't be ordained." Hagan and Purdue fuel one another's anger toward women, and Purdue speaks viciously as he instructs Hagan to preach the morning sermon on "The True Christian Home." "You hit these women hard. Put them in their place. . . . God wants it done now, before this *female* thing gets out of hand." In other words, God wants to crush the women's call for their rightful place of leadership within the Federal Baptist Convention.[8]

But while Hagan and Purdue's violence is usually directed at the women of the convention, they target anyone who disagrees with them. When Excell McBride, the husband of Dorcas, overhears the men belittling his wife, he politely tries to correct them. They mistake him for a drifter with no convention status and have him forcibly removed and beaten senseless. As Dorcas attends to Excell, she reflects upon the violence within the church.

> She remembered reading one time that a cut from stained glass was the most dangerous wound, the hardest to heal. Reflecting on this day, she understood what that meant. At first she was thankful that Excell had been bludgeoned by a bully rather than having been cut by stained glass. But then she became strangely frightened by the thought that the two might be the same.

In the name of Jesus, these power-hungry ministers will violently abuse women and their supporters, male or female, who do not comply with the program. As Dorcas recognizes, the wounds inflicted by the stained-glass church cut the deepest; they take the longest to heal.[9]

The only thing left to happen in this extended parable of a novel is for Dorcas Rose McBride—strong woman, authentic yet simple Christian believer, witness from time to time that the "water in the cistern" of the church has to be changed—to win the presidential election of the Federal Baptist Convention. She does. Then she resigns after reading one brief passage of Scripture to the convention, Matthew 4:8–10 (KJV alt.):

> And the devil, taking Him up into an high mountain, shewed unto Him all the kingdoms of the world in a moment of time. . . . And Jesus answered and said unto Him, Get thee behind Me, Satan: for it is written, Thou shalt worship the Lord thy God, and Him only shalt thou serve.

With that biblical testament ringing in the ears of the conventioneers, Dorcas Rose McBride and her husband, Excell, leave the convention and return to Scotts Grove, Mississippi, and their three foster children, who greet them with "the yelling, hugging, and present-giving that go with a homecoming."[10]

Dorcas Rose McBride plays well the "ideal" role of the minister in the novel. She is a minister without official credentials, but a minister all the same, who shows that while stained glass cuts deep, the love of Jesus Christ heals and makes new.

It's no surprise that many ministers in the South do not appreciate Will Campbell's iconoclastic views of the church and ministry. Some argue that his radically anti-institutional view of Christianity and the ministry is irresponsible. Ministers, they remind us, are representatives of the church, and like it or not, the church is necessarily a human yet divinely authorized institution. Polluted as it is, without the church there would be no faith or ministry. Campbell *might* concede the point, though on any given day with him it is hard to tell. What he wouldn't concede is that that church in its current manifestation, Southern or otherwise, comes anywhere close to approximating the community of servants that Jesus Christ intended when he called the earliest disciples together.

Will Campbell's view of Christian ministry as seen in *The Convention* is sobering. He sounds an alarm to all who will listen (imagine John the Baptist crying in the wilderness) that Christian ministry is being besmirched by slick church politicians and institutional salesman who bank upon fear, nationalism, and the herd instinct of the human population. A quick look around the Southern religious landscape today confirms Campbell's views. Ministers need to be summoned afresh to guard the true calling of the church, for as Dark notes, "It is the vocation of the church to uphold the human as the bearer of the divine image against the drumbeat of nationalism, market devaluing of the human, and every form of mob hysteria." We do serve a kingdom, but it is not the one touted by self-promoting empire builders masquerading as the church. The kingdom of God is inaugurated by a simple servant washing the feet of others and riding upon the back of a donkey. In ministry, that genuine Servant-King is the only one worth measuring ourselves against.[11]

He's on His Way Up: Aiming for the Top
of the Church Ladder in Cassandra King's *The Sunday Wife*

Cassandra King, a native of rural Pickens County, Alabama, recalls that her mother, a devout United Methodist mother, idealized United Methodist ministers. Her mother's high estimation of the ministry clearly played a part in King's decision to marry a United Methodist minister and, as King says, "spend twenty years as a Sunday wife." Her marriage, which ended in disillusionment and divorce, forms the autobiographical backdrop to the novel.[12]

The principal characters in the novel are Dean Lynch; Rev. Dr. Benjamin Lynch, Dean's husband and newly appointed minister of First Methodist Church in Crystal Springs, Florida; and the aristocratic Holderfields, Augusta and Maddox, with whom Dean forms a liberating friendship. King says, "Dean Lynch is not just a preacher's wife; she's the corporate wife, the politician's wife. . . . she's any woman struggling as I did to live up to an unattainable ideal."[13]

Dean Lynch is the story's narrator, and she chronicles her unlikely but deepening bond with the Holderfields and her simultaneous disillusionment with the role of the preacher's wife, a role made particularly difficult because of her husband's ambitious pursuit of ecclesiastical status. Reverend Dr. Benjamin Lynch is "on his way up" to the "top of the ladder of the United Methodist Church." But the higher he climbs, the less willing Dean is to ascend with him.[14]

Being named pastor of Crystal Springs United Methodist Church—prosperous, well attended, and poised for new growth—is Lynch's big break. But Crystal Springs has very traditional role expectations of ministers and their spouses, and Lynch needs a wife who "is her husband's moral equal, his number-one helpmate, unpaid and often unsung." Dean, who comes from a blue-collar and white-trash background, feels ill at ease within middle-class Methodism despite Ben's efforts to make her into a "worthy mate." She becomes her husband's "project" as he attempts to educate Dean "in the ways of the church, molding her to be the perfect preacher's wife."[15]

In a scene realistic enough to make any minister squirm, the couple pulls up for the first time into the driveway of their new parsonage. The welcoming committee peeks out at them from behind the curtains of the house. Anxious to impress the members of the committee, Benjamin preps his wife. "Remember this, because it's *very* important. The Administrative Board chairperson is Bob Harris. Bob Harris, president of First Florida Bank, a real big shot in town, so be especially nice to him." When Dean tries to freshen her appearance in order to dutifully impress the committee, Ben steers her forward, saying, "You don't have time to primp. They're peeking out the windows at us! Let's go." Fueled by Lynch's ambition, the pressure cooker of ministry is already at half steam for Benjamin and Dean Lynch, and they haven't even set foot inside their new parsonage.[16]

Dean does not hide her disdain for her unequal marriage that is driven by her minister husband's ambition. As she reflects upon their circumstances, and how twenty years earlier she had fallen for the young, handsome, and charming minister who would raise her out of backwardness into the bright light of church progress, she says,

> Some cynics say all preachers have God complexes, and Dr. Ben Lynch thought himself a miracle worker. Henry Huggins in a clerical collar, maybe. Since I'd not been schooled in the church, grown up with its traditions and modes of behavior, I lacked all the necessary graces to be the kind of preacher's wife the church expected. So this move was my chance to make a fresh start.

Chafing under Ben's patronizing attitude and exhausted by his corporate ambition, Dean slowly withdraws her support of Ben and his ministry. Ultimately, through divorce, she will break free of Ben's control and derail his career advancement.[17]

Benjamin Lynch's motivation for ministry and ambition are akin to that of Roger Hagan in *The Convention*. He approaches ministry as a "career" rather than a calling: a career with the goal of steady advancement up the ladder of prestige and reward. Though not a Southern fundamentalist like Hagan, Lynch's ministry is similarly shot through with self. Self-advancement, self-adulation, selfish desire infect everything that Lynch touches, particularly his relationship with Dean. The couple does not share the same bedroom because Benjamin prefers to get up all through the night and work on his sermons. Dean must ask permission to come into his bed, yet Benjamin insists that she keep her toiletries on the dresser in their bedroom to "keep up appearances."[18]

When Dean begins to withdraw her support for and cooperation with his ministry, she exposes his narcissism, a narcissism obvious in the inspirational books that he writes on the topic of Christian marriages. "Wives, you will do well to remember that your beloved husband is nothing but a little boy at heart. . . . He longs for your praise and admiration more than anything." Dean finally gets her fill of childishness masquerading as ministerial charm and, unwilling to continue as Ben's "biggest cheerleader," she decides to develop her own friendships outside of the church. Without a submissive Sunday wife to stroke his ego, Benjamin becomes unglued. He retreats further into his own grandiosity and continues to patronize Dean. He coldly informs her that *she* needs therapy and that "things are going to be good for us, if you can just get yourself straightened out." Little wonder that Dean, once she sees daylight, bolts from this boorish marriage.[19]

Reverend Benjamin Lynch is the consummate church manager and politician. "The men respected and liked him; the women in his churches fell in love with him." He is much more concerned about avoiding church conflict than standing by his own convictions. For example, when the broad-minded Holderfields press him to explain his view of modern-day miracles, he takes the safe path. "I have no problem with whatever theory my parishioners embrace. I can relate to both the literalists and the skeptics." Exasperated, Augusta Holderfield replies, "If you ever give up preaching, you could go into politics."[20]

That is precisely what preoccupies Rev. Benjamin Lynch: his political standing within the Annual Conference of the United Methodist Church. His sermons, his publications, his church programs, his recruitment of new members—are all calculated to impress others, particularly the bishop of his area. Getting the bishop's "attention" means one thing to Benjamin Lynch: "He is being groomed for an important job in the bishop's cabinet."[21] Becoming a district superintendent, a member of the bishop's inner circle of conference decision makers, represents the pinnacle of success for Rev. Benjamin Lynch. "Ben had dared not even long for such an appointment, although he'd wanted nothing else." When the appointment to the cabinet occurs, Benjamin explains to the congregation that it is the Lord's will. But Dean cynically considers, "How convenient that the Lord's will coincided with Ben's ambitions."[22]

Lynch is more driven by marketing concerns and his own advancement within the church than authentic ministry among the people. He has fallen prey to vocational idolatry rather than worship of the living God. As Eugene Peterson says in his book on the vocation of ministry, *Under the Unpredictable Plant,* "The idolatry to which pastors are conspicuously liable is not personal but vocational, the idolatry of a religious career that we can take charge of and manage." Encouraged by his peers in ministry and rewarded by a church polity that reinforces career advancement, Benjamin Lynch plays out the role of minister as a corporate manager in pursuit of the good life, American style.[23]

Lynch's blatant positioning for power and status may seem overdrawn to some readers, who may turn away from such a harsh mirror. Clearly King's perspective is based upon her own experience as a "Sunday wife." Another minister in the novel, John Marcus Vickery, actually darkens the image further as a heralded preacher who hides an affair that he had with Augusta Holderfield when she was a teenager (the offense is statutory rape). The affair ultimately destroyed Augusta's faith and life. The Revs. Lynch and Vickery are both emotionally and physically abusive to the women who trust them. Either of them could just as easily have been discussed among the con men and abusers in the ministry in the previous chapter. The image is disgraceful.

But the fact is that among the ranks of ministers in the South, there are scores whose motivations parallel those of Rev. Benjamin Lynch. The genuine work of ministry—proclaiming the gospel, caring for the bereaved, blessing of marriages, and instructing the faithful—are all means to attain personal advancement up the ecclesiastical corporate ladder. "Promotion" almost always equates with appointments to larger-membership churches and greater financial compensation. In leadership deployment, the church mimics corporate America: its ministers serve as branch managers, whose bottom-line results determine reward or punishment in future positions. Excellence in ministry in the North American context usually implies membership growth, expanded buildings, and overall prosperity of the congregation. The true nature of Christian ministry, shaped by the cross and resurrection of Jesus Christ, recedes so far into the shadows as to hardly be perceptible in the lives of those like Benjamin Lynch and Roger Hagan. They have mistaken selfish ambition for gospel commitment and the pursuit of worldly success for the excellence in Christ urged by Paul in the letter to the Philippians, where he says, "Let the same mind be in you that was in Christ Jesus, who, though he was in the form of God did not regard equality with God as something to be exploited, but emptied himself, taking the form of a slave, being born in human likeness" (Philippians 2:5–7).[24] Though some readers will be slow to admit it, Cassandra King has given the ministry a gift in this searing portrait of the ministry in the South. Dean Lynch's voice should warn and haunt ministers who are tempted to substitute themselves for the gospel. She says, "I lost God because I've spent most of life searching in the wrong places."[25]

The majority of ministers, United Methodist and otherwise, are not Benjamin Lynches, but some of us are. Ministry for Lynch is a profession consumed by busyness, pleasing the worldly powers, and craving career advancement no matter what the cost. He is easily recognizable to some of us when we look in the mirror. If the recognition creates shock, perhaps change can follow. After all, who would want to defend a minister who is an ecclesiastical ladder climber, who patronizes his wife, ingratiates himself with the congregation, is self-righteous and unreflective, and is consumed by his own ambition at the cost of his wife's unhappiness and spiritual undoing? He is a minister who shows so little real theological and spiritual awareness that we have no idea what he actually believes about God, Jesus Christ, the church, and

Christian discipleship. Who would want to defend such a minister? Even more, who would want to be him?

It's Almost Wintertime

Doris Bett's short story "Mr. Shawn and Father Scott" features two characters on the margins of Southern small-town respectability: a local eccentric, Mr. Shawn; and the Catholic priest, Father Scott. Spiritual lethargy drags down the ministry of Father Scott, a malaise brought on by the same type of stifling Southern Protestant politics and salesmanship that both Will Campbell and Cassandra King critique. At a meeting of the local ministerial association, dominated by Methodist ministers, Father Scott laments the absence of true religious sentiment among the Protestant boosters who are "faultlessly attired in blue serge with automatic pencils in their shirt pockets." Their campaign to canvass the entire city for Christ leaves the priest cold and downcast. But through persistence and indirection, Mr. Shawn shakes Father Scott out of his stupor. Naming the spiritual vacuum that the testosterone-pumped Protestant campaign obscures, Mr. Shawn observes prophetically, "It will be winter soon."[26]

An overly institutionalized church and an obsessively managed ministry have a chilling effect upon faith. Some segments of the church seem to be frozen in an arctic zone where ministry is deadened or at least on hold. The greening promise of the minister as "pastoral director" that H. Richard Niebuhr proposed in the 1950s in the *The Purpose of the Church and Its Ministry* has petrified into the fixed role of minister as church manager. With the minister as manager, a leadership style taken from business rather than Scripture, all the actions of the minister and the activities of the church became overly scripted. When worship is drained of mystery, when persons (and their giving potential) are calculated like numbers, the demise of authentic faith can't be far behind. And most ironically, this is happening in a culture, the South, that until recently has tried to find its bearings by looking to Christ.[27]

Denying or ignoring the approaching darkness, ministers and the church in the "New South" race into overdrive to keep up with a self-aggrandizing and consumer-crazed culture that lives by slogans, management objectives, and marketing campaigns. Unsure of its purpose, ministry takes on the dominant images of leadership and activity of the surrounding culture. "It's almost wintertime," the Southern fiction writer warns the church and its ministers. But from the hyperactivity of Southern evangelical Protestantism in the early twenty-first century—nailing down the platforms of national politicians with our own religious agendas to constructing megaentertainment-styled sanctuaries—who would ever guess that winter approaches?

Fortunately, John the Baptist continues to roar in the wilderness of the church's cultural captivity. With the return of Advent at the beginning of every Christian year, the church awaits a new word heralded by the prophet who foretells of One who will illumine the darkness. Not all ministers are iced up. Some live by the judgment and promise of the life-giving word of God, who cuts through our grandiose rigidity and shows the way to authentic ministry grounded in him. Following Christ, some ministers arrive with torches lit and axes sharpened to crack the ice of frozen faith. Like young Tarwater in Flannery O'Connor's *The Violent Bear It Away*, God propels some ministers of the South to "GO WARN THE CHILDREN OF GOD OF THE TERRIBLE SPEED OF MERCY."[28]

8

Burning Coals upon Their Lips

The Minister as Prophet

It took us years to get Mr. Chenal to hire black people in the first place. Now after he hires them he don't want to pay them nothing. When we go up there Friday we go'n make it clear. Either he pay the black workers the same he pay the white, or we march before the door.
—Rev. Phillip Martin in Ernest Gaines's *In My Father's House*

I'm L. Ray Flowers. I'm a prophet; I'm a snake. I'm a salad; I'm a steak. I'm a gun; I'm a flower. I'm weakness; I'm power.
—Rev. L. Ray Flowers in Clyde Edgerton's *Lunch at the Piccadilly*

In Zora Neale Hurston's *Jonah's Gourd Vine*, the question is asked, "Ever hear tell of a happy prophet?" The implied negative usually holds true. The prophet is the religious figure who against great resistance seeks to reorient the church and community to its deepest values and identity. He points beyond the present circumstances of human injustice to divine justice yearning to be born. Like Isaiah, when the prophet speaks, "Thus saith the Lord," he announces hope for those who will turn to the Lord and doom for those who will not yield. Happiness for the prophetic minister, if it comes at all, does not come from job satisfaction. It comes from an unswerving obedience to the will of the Lord.[1]

It is a daunting task to balance the prophetic and pastoral in ministry. Many ministers, especially in the white mainline churches of the South, begin their pastoral ministry with prophetic zeal. But no matter how pastoral she is, the minister who challenges current social structures—whether on racial equality, economic justice, militarism, or sexuality—often meets stony silence or aggressive opposition. The job of prophet requires thick skin, a hard head, willingness to move frequently, ability to live off of handouts, and either a remarkably supportive family or no family at all.[2]

It is no surprise, then, that prophets have been in short supply among white Protestant ministers in the South. Here and there a Will Campbell, a Clarence Jordan (the Baptist preacher and founder of the egalitarian Koinonia Farms), or a Myles Horton (the Cumberland

Presbyterian founder of the Highlander School) emerges from within the established white church to become a prophet for the church at large. But their countercultural vision often literally pushes them to the margins of the institutional church, to, for instance, Southwest Georgia, the location of Koinonia Farms; or to the hardscrabble soil of Middle Tennessee, where Will Campbell lives. From a distance, the wider church can then observe the prophet without much threat, as he or she strives to be part of "a demonstration plot for the Kingdom of God." As historian Sam Hill observes, it remains a profound irony that within a region so deeply soaked in the waters of evangelical Christianity, there have been so few prophets and so few "radical communities of faith" that the prophet inspires.[3]

The African American church of the South tells a different story. Unlike their white counterparts, the prophetic ministers of the black church are the most powerful leaders within the African American community as they give witness to radically new social relationships. The black minister as prophet was not only necessary but expected if the African Americans of the South and the country as a whole were ever to claim their God-given dignity and equal rights under the law. Robert Franklin has observed that from the earliest slave preachers, "it was the job of the preachers to lead the people every Sunday through rituals of empowerment that enabled them to resist racism, dismantle legal discrimination, and focus their hopes upon creating a nonracist America." While Martin Luther King Jr. played out the role of black Moses with wider reaching effect than any minister before or since, a host of other black preacher prophets from the South paved the way.[4]

Yet the story is surely more complex than a simple black-and-white designation of ministers as either prophets or conformists. There has always been a handful of white preachers—abolitionists, social gospelers, and civil rights leaders—who have witnessed prophetically on matters of injustice. They have attempted, if not always successfully, to nourish, as Walter Brueggemann says, "a consciousness and perception alternate to the consciousness and perception of the dominant culture around us." They have struggled to discover how to effectively challenge a system while simultaneously standing within it.[5]

At the same time, some black ministers of the South have been slow to enact a prophetic ministry, and for good reason. The stakes are always higher in the South for the outspoken black minister and the black citizenry. The black prophet in the South raises his vision of a new heaven and earth at the risk of his own life and his family's, the safety of his community, and the value of his property. This is still true in some sections of the South today. And during the civil rights era, not all black preachers were willing or able to engage the struggle in the same way. The risk was too great. Some, including Martin Luther King Sr., saw the direct-action tactics of his son as misguided, even as he embraced the goal of racial justice.[6]

It's not surprising, then, that the image of the minister as prophet in Southern literature reflects this cultural and racial divide. Courageous, prophetic, even militant pictures emerge in fiction of the African American ministers of the South. But their white counterparts lack the prophetic fire to speak truth to power. Economically dependent upon their churches' powerful members, the white-establishment ministers provide religious legitimacy for the perpetuation of the social sins of the South, especially the "original sin" of racism. While racism of today may not be as violent and overt as it was during the Jim Crow South, it continues in the form of white privilege within many institutions. Ministers are often just as reluctant to engage contemporary white privilege as they were to engage Jim Crow segregation. Sadly, when listening to white ministers of the South, the writer usually hears the same thing that Martin Luther King Jr. heard from his cell in the Birmingham jail: "A weak ineffectual voice with an uncertain sound."[7]

Yet if we search, tucked within the pages of Southern literature, we can find the occasional prophet. Most of these literary prophets, not surprisingly, are concerned about race relations in the South, but some of them confront other injustices that stalk the region. Occasionally we find those rare fictional ministers who whether on matters of racism, economic justice, gender, or age discrimination, in the words of William Faulkner, courageously "speak now against the day" when someone will say, "Why didn't someone tell us this before?" They help us to see the challenges of prophetic ministry in the South, and they show us the humanity of the prophet whose vision always runs ahead of reality.[8]

Changed Just about Everything Round Here: A Prophet Without Honor in Ernest Gaines's *In My Father's House*

In My Father's House takes place in the bayou country of south-central Louisiana, in the fictional town of St. Adrienne, a setting similar to where author Ernest Gaines spent most of his childhood years. It's 1970, two years after the assassination of Martin Luther King Jr., and Rev. Phillip Martin is the sixty-year-old pastor of Solid Rock Baptist Church.

A skilled preacher and pastor, Rev. Martin is a widely respected, prophetic leader within the black community. The similarites between Rev. Phillip Martin and Martin Luther King Jr. are intentional. As the local boardinghouse owner, Mrs. Virginia Colar, says about him, "He's our civil rights leader around here. . . . Done such a good job here, people thinking 'bout sending him on to Washington. . . . Changed just about everything round here." Like so many black ministers in the South during the civil rights era, he actively organizes the black community to pursue civil rights within their town, and he eloquently nurtures their God-given vision of justice for all.[9]

The challenge facing Rev. Martin and the black community is that the white merchant, Chenal, "won't pay the colored nothing for working." Martin and other church leaders organize a boycott of Chenal's store. As Martin says to the congregation,

> It took us years to get Mr. Chenal to hire black people in the first place. Now after he hires them he don't want to pay them nothing. When we go up there Friday we go'n make it clear. Either he pay the black workers the same he pay the white, or we march before the door.

The people follow Martin's prophetic leadership because through him they hear the sounds of freedom and with him they see a way to get there.[10]

All is not smooth sailing for Martin, however. He ministers to a black church and community in the South that is on the verge of losing focus in the waning years of the civil rights movement. He tries to stay the course set in the mid-1950s by continuing to advocate for nonviolent direct action as the best strategy to wrest justice from the white power structure. But Rev. Martin's prophetic witness is not enough for many of the younger generation, who challenge him on his nonviolent approach to social change. The black minister as prophet, even among his own people in the South, who need his leadership, is sometimes "without honor," and we see this when an activist/militant says to Rev. Martin, "Shit. . . . There ain't nothing in them churches, Pops, but more separation." Like prophetic ministers today, Martin must lead the community toward greater justice while simultaneously answering those who criticize his goals and methods.[11]

But the most vexing complication for Martin comes from his past, which arrives in the angry and haunting stares of Robert X, who is at

first mistaken for a drifter. In reality, though, Robert is Martin's unacknowledged son from a secret relationship that had ended more than
twenty years earlier, when Martin refused to take responsibility for
Robert or for his other two children with Robert's mother, Johanna.
After Martin abandoned Johanna and the children, she moved to Cali-
fornia, but she was forced to support herself as a prostitute; Robert's
brother went to prison for violent crimes, and his sister was sexually
abused. Martin never attempted to contact Johanna or send assistance,
and Robert returns to St. Adrienne to confront his father and to seek
revenge "for destroying me. For making me the eunuch I am. For
destroying my family: my mama, my brother, my sister." Robert wants
to make his father pay for the years of hardship, neglect, and abuse that
the family has endured. Defiantly, he says to Martin, "I wanted to come
here and kill you."[12]

Ironically, it was the same racism that Martin now so actively opposes
as a Christian minister that caused his separation from his first son.
Racism eviscerated Martin's ability to care for his own family. Weeping
as he talks, Martin tries to explain to Robert why he abandoned him
and the rest of the family.

> I was paralyzed. Paralyzed . . . I had legs, but I couldn't move. I had
> arms, but I couldn't lift them up to you. It took a man to do these
> things, and I wasn't a man. I was just some other brutish animal who
> could cheat, steal, rob, kill—but not stand. Not be responsible. Not
> protect you or your mother. They had branded that in us from the
> time of slavery.

The knife of racism, driven deep into the bodies and psyche of the
Southern black, divides father from son. This is painfully apparent
when Robert is arrested for loitering and Rev. Martin appeals to the
white sheriff to release him from jail on bond. The sheriff forces Martin to admit that Robert is his son, but when he makes the admission,
the sheriff mockingly heaps coals upon the minister's head: "Look to me
like he ought to be in his father's house."[13]

Two forces—love for family and desire for justice—meet and collide
in Martin's life. In order to secure Robert's release from jail, he is forced
to call off the protest against Chenal's store; the sheriff will only release
Robert if Martin cancels the protest. The prophet and father is torn
between his commitments to the people and God and his desire to be
reconciled with his son. "I can't take from them people what they been

working for for so long. We just about changed everything in this town—except Chenal. He's the only one still holding out, the only one won't go along. I can't do that to my people." The enforcer of white power has the prophet of black freedom exactly where he wants him: Choose the movement and deny your son; choose your son and deny the movement. "Well you want him or not?" the sheriff demands. "I don't have all day."[14]

Martin agrees, but to no good end. Not only does Robert view Martin's abandonment of the march with contempt, but the civil rights committee members question his integrity. When he finally confesses to them and his wife his secret paternity, they remove him from his leadership of the committee, for as one member says, "No one person can come before the cause, Reverend. Not even you." Phillip Martin cannot escape the burden of the past. He strives to provide leadership for the people in the present and future only to run smack into the wall of the past.

Here is the harsh reality for all Christian ministers, but it is especially glaring for prophetic ministers within the conservative South. The prophet's message runs far ahead of his or her own ability to embody it. Even as Phillip Martin pushes for social justice, his own unjust behavior comes back to haunt him. The prophet's feet are surely made of clay like all the rest of humanity. And the more effective the prophet is at pushing society toward God's beloved community, the more eagerly the public notes his flaws. Any minister who seeks to initiate social change, no matter how small or large the endeavor, should be ready for the public scrutiny that will follow.[15]

Some prophets can bear the burden of the past better than others. In Rev. Phillip Martin's case, the shame of his past nearly destroys him and his ministry. When released from jail, Robert disappears, so Phillip decides to search for him. Martin's wife, Alma, tries to reason with him:

> Ever since I met you, Phillip, you been running, running, and running. Away from what Phillip? Trying to make up for what Phillip? For what you did to that boy? For what you did to his mon? For other things you did in the past? The past is the past, Phillip. You can't make up for the past.

But he will not listen to Alma. He is desperate to set things right with his estranged son.[16]

After a frantic search for Robert, the novel concludes with Martin learning from Alma and several of his church members that Robert has turned his anger upon himself and committed suicide by hanging himself from a railroad trestle. "That's not so, that's not so. . . . God knows that's not so," Martin laments. Devastated by his son's death and unable to ever be reconciled with him, Martin lies on the bed in despair and repeats to his wife, "I'm lost, Alma. I'm lost."[17]

As Martin alternates between self-hatred, denial of God, and feelings of hopelessness about himself and his call, Beverly, a member of the congregation and family friend, raises the voice of the people. "You have to go back . . . To your wife, your children, your church. Even to the ones back there who don't have faith in anything." Martin protests that he cannot return because he has lost all faith, that God has failed to reward him for his faithful leadership. But Beverly challenges him:

> Can't you see how many times He's rewarded you? . . . The ones you led to that courthouse, to that fountain, don't tremble any more when they lean over to get a drink of water. Isn't that payment enough? . . . I take my class there, and they walk all through that courthouse without trembling. . . . Isn't that payment enough, Reverend Martin?

Then Beverly reminds Martin, the prophet, that while his ministry cannot change the past, it can surely change the future. "You wanted the past changed, Reverend Martin. . . . Even He can't do that. So that leaves nothing but the future. We work toward the future. That's all we work for, isn't it?"[18]

Phillip Martin, the broken man and defeated prophet, will have to decide like so many tragic figures in ministry and Southern literature if the sins of the past will foreclose the future. The prophet who on behalf of the people was always "ready to get the first blow" has been struck down by his own past moral failures, even if those personal sins arose because of the far-greater evil of slavery. Beverly and Alma, the feminine voices of resilience and hope, whisper to the wounded leader the final words of the novel, "We just go'n have to start again."[19]

Whether Phillip Martin can "start again" is a question only the reader and the prophetic ministers of the South can truly answer. Gaines's *In My Father's House* casts in high relief the excruciating tensions within the life of the minister as prophet. If not inevitable, it is almost axiomatic that the minister deeply moved by a vision of social justice will unintentionally create pain and suffering for one's own family. The cost of a truly prophetic ministry is high enough that if the prophet could fully count it in advance, one might, Moses-like, do everything possible to reject God's call. Prompted by prophetic vision, Phillip Martin—like many Southern ministers, black and white—has come to that crossroads in ministry where he will emerge from the war between his soul and God with a renewed vision for the future or with a concession to defeat. He knows that the church and community of the South are both ready to champion him and to crucify him.

This image of the African American prophetic minister in the South challenges those of conscience to continue to wrestle with the monstrous entanglements, past and present, of race and religion in the South. Never perfect, and even in weakness, the black prophetic minister points the Southern church and culture, indeed the nation as a whole, toward God's new day of just and loving relationships.

Prophetic Ministry and Race Relations Today

Among the Southern stories and novels of the past ten to fifteen years, few treat the theologically and socially charged theme of religion and race through the character of the contemporary minister. Moreover, most look back, in the manner of Ernest Gaines, at either the civil rights struggle of the 1960s or at the earlier decades of the Jim Crow era, ignoring problems of race that exist today.[20]

It is as if our writers no longer see the church or its ministers in that part of the Southern story that narrates race. Why does the Southern prophet of race relations appear primarily as a character from the past? And what does this suggest to us about ministry in the South today?

First, the subject of race and religion is no longer perceived as the defining issue for the South. As Linda Wagner-Martin points out, writing about religion and race in the South is no longer "fashionable." This obscures the fact that racism hangs on in the South and within its religious institutions, even if many whites do not want to see it. But there has been, largely because of the gains of the civil rights movement, a reduction of the black-white racial contention in the South, a conflict that has riveted its writers and exercised the conscience of its religious leaders, whether those leaders were defending the unjust social relations of the old South or actively advocating for change in the "New South."[21]

At the same time, other minority groups are introducing new cultural elements to the Southern racial situation. Over the past twenty years, the influx of Hispanics and Asians into the cultural stew of the

South has radically altered the Southern landscape in ways that many whites and blacks are only beginning to perceive, especially when it comes to religious practices.[22]

Black and white church groups in the South seem to be focusing their attention elsewhere than upon racial reconciliation. While the historic Protestant mainline denominations in the South, black and white, such as the National Baptists, the United Methodist Church, the Christian Methodist Episcopal (CME) Church, and the Presbyterian Church (U.S.A.) continue to advocate for just racial relations at all levels of church and society, the battle has shifted to sexuality, specifically the question of ordination and marriage of homosexuals. The historic African American denominations in the South (Baptist, AME [African Methodist Episcopal], AME Zion, CME), originally at the vanguard of the civil rights struggle, and the newer independent (many of which are Black megachurches) and Pentecostal groups (e.g., COGIC [Church of God in Christ]) continue to gain economic and political clout in ways that deflect the issue of racial injustice and highlight membership growth, personal empowerment, personal morality, and the long-denied pursuit of economic prosperity, matters that have preoccupied the white churches for generations.

Second, the right wing of American religious life, with especially strong footholds in the South, has shifted the region's religious concerns away from the progressive social agenda of the civil rights era and has, ironically, used social activism, as Paul Harvey argues, "not so much to pull a backward region forward as to reclaim a 'lost' heritage of a once supposedly 'Christian America.'" Attention to racism in the South has become diffuse because the political ground has shifted so dramatically since 1980. Conservative Christians in the South, without regard to color or denomination, have joined hands on the politically charged issues of abortion and homosexuality. The faith-based initiatives of the Bush administration have proved popular among both conservative white evangelicals and historically liberal black churches, creating new alliances between blacks and whites in the South that both mitigate and paper over existing racial injustice.[23]

With all these baffling religious and political hurdles, the minister like the writer may be vexed about where to take hold. Writer Jonathan Franzen claims that it is hard now to write a novel of "social importance" when the face of the society in question shifts as quickly as the click of a mouse. The same can be said about ministry.[24]

Nevertheless, ministers cannot afford to let the church ignore the ongoing challenge of race relations in the South. Civil laws are now firmly in place that prohibit racial discrimination and support equal justice for all. But it is at the level of communal interaction where the Christian church will either advance or set back racial understanding. In the sanctuary, around the communion table, at the potluck dinner—these are the places where the minister and the congregation either do or do not concretely demonstrate a prophetic and pastoral commitment to racial reconciliation. Moreover, with a quickly expanding multicultural South, the challenge is even greater for the church to help foster a culture where racial difference does not divide and where in our laws and religious practices we respect the common humanity of all.

Southern church and society await prophetic ministers who will tackle the newest twists on the old theme of religion and race. In the years ahead the church will look to ministers who with vision and compassion can carry us toward genuine reconciliation beneath the contemporary veneer of a booming South, a South that is daily more characterized by closer proximity between races but, for all Southern religion's talk of reconciliation, may be no closer to genuine communion.

Beyond the prophetic minister engaged with race relations, Southern writers occasionally track other prophets among us. These prophets work along different margins of Southern society, reorienting us to Christianity's deepest values. We will now briefly meet one such minister in the work of Clyde Edgerton.

Why Should Churches and Nursing Homes Not Be Interchangeable? Relieving the Suffering of Old Folks at Homes in Clyde Edgerton's *Lunch at the Piccadilly*

Reverend L. Ray Flowers, former roving Pentecostal evangelist and amateur country music player, stirs things up at the Rosehaven Convalescence Center in fictional Listre, North Carolina. Clyde Edgerton's quick rhyming, two-timing retired evangelist has temporarily landed in the nursing home to receive physical therapy for a knee that was nearly bitten off by sharks while surf fishing off the Outer Banks in North Carolina. To his physical therapist, Faye, he eagerly recounts his days as a ranging evangelist in the Midwest, where he put the "pedal to the metal, a-healing and a-squealing, a-touching and a-feeling." To anyone who will listen to the opening of his down-home and word-giddy sermons, he announces himself as "L. Ray Flowers. I'm a prophet; I'm a snake.

I'm a salad; I'm, a steak. I'm a gun; I'm a flower. I'm weakness. I'm power." Rev. L. Ray Flowers is an unlikely prophet who, when he gets a good look at the "wrecks of old women lining the grim halls of nursing homes," launches into action to form a worldwide movement to unite churches and nursing homes to relieve the tedium and suffering of the elderly: "It shall be called Nurches of America, Chursing Homes of the United States."[25]

This manic would-be liberator of the "old folks at homes" is only a few steps shy of crazy. Audacious yet sensitive, talented yet profligate, he zings from concern for the elderly in the nursing home ("I like Mr. Flowers. He pays attention to everybody") to composing wickedly funny prayers before lunch at the Piccadilly—for the preservation of Southern foods and the improvement of Southern race relations:

> "Oh, the dying and bygone potential union of blacks and rednecks,
> . . . now frayed beyond repair and only redeemable in the fading mist
> of this new century, redeemable through cabbage, collards, turnip
> salet, fried fatback, the slunken foods now reserved for movies and
> poverty."

With such paeans to Southern culture and his zany proposal to merge churches with nursing homes, L. Ray Flowers is the real McCoy of independent, Southern religious eccentrics whose juiced-up prophetic sermons get the arthritic hands of the elderly clapping and their wheelchairs rolling.[26]

What makes him appealing as a prophetic minister is that coursing right along with his bodacious wordplay in sermons is a genuine concern for the elderly residents of Rosehaven Convalescence Center. He may sound like a hip-hopping minister on crack, but he delivers a social punch on behalf of senior citizens that keeps the nursing home residents listening and following. As William Willimon observes, "The Holy Spirit produces uppity speech." L. Ray preaches like Muhammad Ali used to taunt: "Float like a butterfly, sting like a bee."

> Boogie-woogie glory be to every whap-whop jack-junkie honky-
> punkie snip-snap-snay foy-fey lard bucket caught in the grip of
> greed. Shout it out. Strike down, O Lord God, Jerry Falwell and Pat
> Robertson, Jimmy Swaggart and Norman Vincent Peale. All the TV
> preachers in the land, sentimental slobs who have called on the
> syrup of sweetness to suck up money from the more sentimental
> than they are.

L. Ray follows this warm-up riff on the crass materialism and manipulation of TV evangelists with the manifesto for the new nursing home movement:

> We are about to pronounce the grand fact that nursing homes and churches all across this land must become interchangeable. Why do we need a church house for Christians to visit on Sunday mornings when we've got nursing homes for Christians to visit? Christians sitting in churches while nursing homes sit around the corner is wrong!

To that pronouncement, the elderly residents shout, "Amen. That's what I said."[27]

Yes, the proposal is preposterous, as preposterous as any prophetic proposal to envision a new heaven and earth from the peaceable kingdom of Isaiah to the Holy City of the New Jerusalem. But L. Ray Flowers the prophet is not bound by what is probable; rather, he pronounces what in God's good world will "gladden the wrecks" of the elderly in nursing homes across America. His words can boldly name the new way, and in that holy boldness the sermons of L. Ray Flowers begin to create the very thing they name.[28]

Edgerton has said, "I wanted L. Ray to be lively and different from most evangelists. . . . So he was free to preach whatever was on his mind." As we see, what he preaches is gospel (good news) for the elderly residents of the Rosehaven Convalescence Center.[29]

With his ability to help believers construct an alternative world, L. Ray Flowers does not so much mirror Southern ministry as show us the ministry as it could be. Therein lies the power of the fictional ministers in general and L. Ray Flowers in particular. He does not take to the streets as an activist or civil rights organizer, the more recognizable Southern prophetic ministers. Rather, L. Ray's prophetic zeal keeps hope alive, even among the rejected elderly. As Willimon suggests, "Our prophetic preaching has as its goal the evocation of prophetic schoolteachers, shopkeepers, nursing home residents, and sixteen-year-olds who can speak the truth to power." Flowers's vision of a new church, a church where the elderly always count, turns the ministry of the church with the elderly from funeral chaplaincy to a daily banquet at the Piccadilly, where the decrepitudes of old age are smothered in gravy and spiced with hard-won wit and wisdom.[30]

It may seem an unlikely place for a prophetic ministry—the nursing homes of North America. But given the growing institutionalizing of the elderly and the lack of adequate insurance and medical care for them, the "convalescent homes" may be just the place where a new kind of prophetic ministry needs to take root. Scattered all across the South are senior care "homes" that are the latest version of social slums. There we warehouse the least desirable and less financially solvent of our senior citizens. The abuses of the elderly that occur in some of these facilities is unconscionable. The death of dignity that occurs before the physical death of the elderly is inhumane.

A prophetic ministry for the aged will remind the church of its long-standing respect for the elderly and will combine personal care with social action. It will call for bold preaching and hardheaded political negotiation while remembering the needs of the elderly for daily touch, comfort, respect, and laughter. Some senior care homes provide all of this and more for their residents. But many senior citizens, usually those without the ability to pay, are marooned in squalid conditions, near comatose from drug-induced sedation, and shunted off behind closed doors, where they babble as they roll themselves aimlessly down dingy corridors, waiting for some kind of contact from an overworked and underpaid staff member. The prophetic minister cannot allow the church to forget these oldest members of the human family nor cease to encourage us to care for them with the love and respect that they deserve. Even as she extends care to them, she will agitate for the kind of social policies that will make it possible for all elderly citizens to live their final years in safety and dignity.

Here Am I—Send Me

Reflecting upon ministry in today's culture, Walker Percy says that the church "will be seen increasingly as what it was in the beginning, a saving remnant, a sign of contradiction, a stumbling block, a transcultural phenomenon, a pilgrim church." The priest and prophets who serve this church and God's world are bearers of the good news and have the distinctive challenge to speak it "with such authenticity that it can penetrate the most exhausted hearing, revive the most jaded language."[31]

Gaines, Edgerton, and Percy remind the Southern church and its ministry to recall its own prophetic tradition. Surely God's prophetic voice still sounds within the Christian ministry. Surely Protestant and Catholic ministers alike can still hear the voice that shakes the foundations of the temple and knocks the quaking recipients upon their knees, only to rise again in obedience to stammer out, "Here am I, send me." These fictional prophets show us in startlingly fresh ways that service of the crucified Savior is risky business. No one can protect the faithful minister from the dangers of the cross, least of all the prophetic minister.

The prophetic voice not only sounds the alarm to wake us from a culturally induced torpor, but also shows us the way to live faithfully in an age of routine violence, exploitative materialism, subterranean racism, and spiritual deception—in short, a voice that will help us name and confront evil in all its guises. It is a voice that the church desperately needs to hear. As William Willimon cautions, "It is a sure sign of a compromised church—a church that has retired from the battle with the principalities and powers, a church without prophets—when one finds a church that has stopped dealing with sin."[32]

To be honest, it is doubtful that on matters of racial, economic, gender, age, or environmental justice the Southern church will any more *willingly* heed the prophets of today than of yesterday. But the novelist, who through the fictional prophet prods the church toward recognition of its own failures to follow the crucified Savior, is at least sowing seeds of hope among church and culture. When the genuine prophet arises among us, perhaps we will be less eager to stone and kill him. In some rare instances, by the prodding of the prophet, the church may miraculously become more the church that Christ sets within the world: an agent and sign of God's liberating love for all humanity.

9

Signs Will Follow Them That Believe

The Minister as Misfit and Mystic

> What I mean to have you know is: I'm no goddam preacher. I preach the
> Church without Christ. I'm member and preacher to that church where
> the blind don't see and the lame don't walk and what's dead stay that way.
> —Hazel Motes in Flannery O'Connor's *Wise Blood*

> "How do I know you are the Lord talking and not the Devil?" and God
> said, "I will give you this sign." Then lo the darkness gave way to sun-
> light, and there in the middle of the road appeared a dazzling white ser-
> pent, and Daddy was anointed to walk over there and pick it up, and it
> grew tame as a toy in his arms. "Now go forth and spread my word,"
> God told Daddy, and this was the true start of Daddy's ministry.
> —Florida Grace Shepherd in Lee Smith's *Saving Grace*

If the prophetic minister waging battle against the powers and principalities does not arouse Southerners from spiritual malaise, perhaps one
or the other of his nearest kin, the misfit or mystic, will. Mainstream
Christians easily dismiss these out-of-the-box ministers who haunt the
margins of Southern society. In our inner cities and remote mountain
settlements, they shout their cockeyed view of the gospel to anyone who
will listen or to no one at all. But these wildly unpredictable servants of
the Lord, whether handling snakes in the name of Jesus or preaching
from the hood of an automobile, can plug the religiously apathetic back
into the supercharged mystery of God, the One who answers, if anyone
dares to ask, "I AM WHO I AM" (Exodus 3:14).

In the photograph album of characters from Southern fiction, the
religious misfit stands out like a spooky, laser-eyed half cousin. Erratic
and prone to spiritual theatrics, the misfit is long on apocalyptic pro-
nouncements and short on reason. Often self-ordained or defrocked,
the misfit scatters abroad an idiosyncratic gospel that most mainline
Christians reject. He invites stereotyping.

But the minister as misfit is not simply fodder for Southern religious
stereotype. From the rich soil of Southern fundamentalism, religious
oddballs do spring up. The misfit predictably emerges from an over-
heated religious environment that encourages spiritual fervor; the difference is that his exuberance for all things religious, particularly the
Bible and preaching, frequently reaches a fevered pitch that, strangely,

both attracts and repels everyone within earshot. His extremism drives others away from the very gospel that he authoritatively proclaims, but to the religious misfit, fidelity to his own brand of the gospel is all that counts. Without family who will claim him, economically destitute, and hot with religious zeal, the misfit minister wanders throughout Southern communities preaching to passersby on street corners and in public parks, or he retreats into his own deteriorating dwelling to talk to God, the ghosts of his past, or to the television. To many, he is a freak. Defending the prevalence of such freakish religious characters, Flannery O'Connor quipped, "Whenever I am asked why Southern writers particularly have a penchant for writing about freaks, I say it is because we are still able to recognize one."[1]

Ironically, the religious misfit "fits" because of the religious fervor that still grips the region. As O'Connor said, "I think it is safe to say that while the South is hardly Christ-centered, it is most certainly Christ-haunted." For proof, we need look no further than the street corners of our own cities and the mushrooming of churches in the South today. In a storied region still shadowed by the cross, whether in fact or fiction, the misfit minister is sure to play a role.[2]

The minister as mystic cuts a slightly different path across the Southern religious landscape. Evelyn Underhill defined mysticism as "the direct intuition or experience of God; and a mystic is a person who has, to a greater or less degree, such a direct experience—one whose religion and life are centered not merely on an accepted belief or practice, but on that which he regards as first-hand personal knowledge." Like the misfit, the mystic frequently dwells on the margins of social and religious respectability in the South. The mystic too is a liminal character whose spiritual eccentricities fascinate and repel.[3]

Unlike the misfit, however, the mystic often stirs up a following. Whether contemplative pilgrims steadily streaming to Thomas Merton's monastic cabin or the enthusiast listening to the ecstatic sermon of a Pentecostal firebrand, the mystic's charismatic powers of speech, vision, discernment, and healing draw in the spiritually starved, believers who hunger and thirst for the experience of God, especially in its more supernatural manifestations. A devout clarity guides the mystic as she personally responds to the Spirit-filled promptings of God, frequently called "signs." In the observation of William James, the mystic overcomes "all the usual barriers between the individual and the Absolute." Thus, the true mystic usually winds up being followed by a devout crowd, despite one's own leanings toward religious retreat.[4]

Southern writers regularly mine these extraordinary veins of Christian ministry, sometimes lampooning the quirks of the misfit or the ecstasies of the mystic, or in other instances prizing the mystic's spiritual depth or the misfit's countercultural stance. Scripture shouts that Jewish and Christian faith is far from safe; meeting God is wildly unpredictable. After all, the original mystic Moses talks with burning bushes. The misfit prophet Elijah's only friends are ravens. Peter has ecstatic visions that presage unity among Jews and Gentiles. And Jesus, himself a misfit and mystic, follows the Holy Spirit into the wilderness to do battle with demons and—in identification with all the outcasts of the world—to be tortured and isolated upon a cross. In their spiritual directness the misfit and the mystic take us close to the divine wildness that beats at the heart of religion.

We now turn to two ministers from Southern fiction who put flesh upon these claims. Hazel Motes, misfit minister of Flannery O'Connor's *Wise Blood*, spews an antigospel message with such venom that only other misfits can sense the suppressed hunger for righteousness that drives him on. Reverend Virgil Shepherd, in Lee Smith's *Saving Grace*, would hardly call himself a mystic. He'd say he is just a simple minister "follering the plan of God." But when in the height of religious fervor he reaches down to take up a rattlesnake, all bets are off.[5]

If You've Been Redeemed, I Wouldn't Want to Be: Ministry in the Church Without Christ in Flannery O'Connor's *Wise Blood*

Hazel Motes, the protagonist of O'Connor's first novel, *Wise Blood*, is stung by Christian faith at a young age. There is no escaping his circuit-riding preacher grandfather, "a waspish old man who had ridden over three counties with Jesus hidden in his head like a stinger." This hellfire-and-damnation preacher drags young Motes along as he makes his circuit in East Tennessee, preaching from the hood of his Ford, using Motes as an illustration of the extremes to which Jesus will go to save the lost: "Did they know that even for that boy there, for that mean sinful unthinking boy standing there with his dirty hands clenching and unclenching at his sides, Jesus would die ten million deaths before He would let him lose his soul?" Like a drill, his grandfather bores religion into Motes. Little wonder that by the age of twelve, the religious die is cast within the soul of this Southern Protestant fundamentalist.[6]

Motes grows up with the certain knowledge that he is, in O'Connor's phrase, "Christ-haunted" even if not "Christ-centered." The Jesus that Motes will serve is no gentle shepherd, no peacemaking Savior. Rather, a frightening, unpredictable Christ haunts Motes, implanted within him by his severe grandfather and his devout mother. As an adolescent, he sees "Jesus move from tree to tree in the back of his mind, a wild ragged figure motioning him to turn around and come off into the dark where he was not sure of his footing, where he might be walking on the water and not know it and then suddenly know it and drown." This ominous Jesus exerts an unrelenting force upon young Motes. He hovers in the shadows of Motes's consciousness, creating fear and guilt and an exacting obedience. There is no relief from the harsh judgment of the demanding Savior and the burdensome guilt that pursues him.[7]

Motes joins the army during World War II, but he never fits in. Other soldiers mock his devotion so severely that he tries to cast off faith. "They told him he didn't have any soul, . . . and he saw the opportunity to be converted to nothing instead of to evil."[8] When he returns after the war to the burgeoning, "New South," he discovers that his hometown of Eastrod, Tennessee, is dried up, his parents have died, and he is alone in the world.

As he journeys by train from Eastrod to the modern city of Taulkingham, Motes's appearance is strikingly odd. He wears a "stiff black broad-brimmed hat, . . . a hat that an elderly country preacher would wear." His suit is a glaring blue with the price tag "still stapled on the sleeve of it." Motes's eyes are the color of pecan shells set within deep sockets. He has a nose "like a shrike's bill and a long vertical crease on either side of his mouth." His hair appears to be permanently flattened by the heavy hat. All in all, Motes looks the part of a seriously underfunded, crude evangelist who just might have blood on his hands. His fellow travelers are either puzzled by Motes's appearance or disdainful of his coarse mannerisms and his rude outbursts. For example, an elderly lady on the train, Mrs. Hitchcock, simply doesn't know how to respond when, after she tries to make small talk with Motes, he turns on her and blurts, "I reckon you think you been redeemed."[9]

Motes arrives in Taulkingham angry at God and the world and determined to reject his Christian faith. He cannot shake the primitive Jesus bequeathed to him by his family, but he gives it an awful try, doing everything within his power to cast off the fear, as O'Connor says about Southerners in general, that "he may have been formed in the image and likeness of God." Since he cannot make peace with Jesus, Motes tries to violently reject him. To anyone who will listen, he claims, "Nothing matters but that Jesus don't exist."[10]

A misfit preacher without a congregation, Motes stands on the hood of his rattletrap automobile, parked outside of a movie house, and launches into impromptu sermons filled with anti-Christian vitriol.

> I preach the Church Without Christ. I'm a member and preacher to that church where the blind don't see and the lame don't walk and what's dead stays that way. Ask me about that church and I'll tell you it's the church that the blood of Jesus don't foul with redemption.

When passersby respond to him at all, it is with disdain. But this only spurs Hazel to greater fervor. "My church is the Church Without Christ, lady. . . . If there's no Christ, there's no reason to have a set place to do it in."[11]

Ironically, in his fierce repudiation of all outward forms and dogmas of Christian religion, Hazel begins to draw near to Jesus Christ, or at least to an authentic search for Christ. The crowning action in the story comes when Motes blinds himself by putting quicklime in his eyes, wrapping himself in barbed wire, and dropping glass in his shoes as he wanders around the city. A misfit Christian ascetic, he stumbles into a ditch and dies.

Having faced the folly of his denials of Christ, Motes blinds himself to signal new spiritual sight. O'Connor's symbolism calls to mind not only the Greek tragedy *Oedipus Rex*, but also Mark's story of the blind Bartimaeus who "sees" that Jesus is the Messiah, Son of David (Mark 10:46–52). It further alludes to Matthew's account of the lame who walk and the blind who see (Matthew 15:29–31), and it echoes the most beloved of all evangelical hymns, "Amazing Grace." Motes's self-imposed blindness, along with wrapping himself in barbed wire and placing glass in his shoes, is certainly a form of penance because he recognizes that he is "not clean." But his self-imposed Christian asceticism suggests Hazel's new awareness that the Christian life is a journey toward God rather than self.

At the end of the story, Motes enters into the mystery of faith where "the eyes are closed—but they are also opened." Mrs. Flood, Motes's landlady, says that "even when he was sitting motionless in a chair, his face had the look of straining toward something." What he strains for is that "pin point of light" that beckons out in the darkness. It is the light that the blind Hazel now sees because, as he says, "if there's no bottom in your eyes, they hold more." In his twisted, even tortured witness to that light, Hazel may even have gained his first true disciple in Mrs. Flood, who in looking at the blind Hazel has "an intimation of something hidden near her but out of her reach." She wonders, when Hazel dies in the ditch, if "she had finally got to the beginning of something she couldn't begin."[12]

O'Connor's misfit minister shows us the grace-infused distortions that serious submission to the cross of Jesus Christ can provoke. Hazel Motes cannot be mistaken for the institutionally bound and self-serving ministers that appear in, for example, Cassandra King's *The Sunday Wife* or Will Campbell's *The Convention*. A severe grace pursues O'Connor's misfit. Hard as he might try, Motes cannot escape the burden of choice between accepting or rejecting God's grace. Once captured by grace, there is no safety—only submission to the terrible freedom of God. As O'Connor says, "That belief in Christ is to some a matter of life and death has been a stumbling block for readers who would prefer to think it a matter of no great consequence." But for Motes, Christ bends him all out of shape and makes him into a character who in the end gives disturbing witness to the holy madness of redemption.[13]

Hazel Motes's ministry cannot be evaluated in conventional terms. Hazel gives evangelical witness in words and deeds, extreme though they are, to the transforming nature of the Christian gospel. The cross of Christ is lodged so deeply within Hazel's gut that the more he tries to deny it, the more it scores him from the inside out. Among the faithless citizens and spiritual imposters of Taulkingham, Hazel blazes like a tortured saint. We, like the citizens of Taulkingham, discount his blunt prophetic utterances and recoil at his ascetic self-lacerations because we much prefer a homogenized Christian experience that goes down smooth and easy.

One problem in Christian ministry specifically and Christian faith in general is that many in our secularized society do not see the homogenization of faith as the problem. At least that seems to be what Hazel Motes screams off the page. Mesmerized by technology, stupefied by materialism ("Nobody with a good car needs to be justified," Motes says), reassured by comfortable religion, we see Motes's ultimate penance and extreme mortification as barbaric. But pursued first by the devil and then by God, his body and mind are a battleground for truth. As O'Connor says regarding the high stakes of Christian faith, and quoting St. Cyril of Jerusalem in instructing catechumens, "The dragon sits by the side of the road, watching those who pass. Beware lest he devour you. We go to the Father of Souls, but it is necessary to pass by the dragon." Hazel Motes meets his fair share of dragons in Taulking-ham: liars, cheats, prostitutes, and thieves (ourselves), with whom he must do battle. In the end, this Southern misfit becomes a Christian minister in spite of himself. [14]

We can dismiss Hazel Motes's misshapen ministry as weird beyond belief, but we do so by denying the cost of Christian commitment. Hazel Motes, a misfit by most everyone's standards, bears witness that Christian faith and baptism bring about a life-shattering break with the old order of the fallen world. "I have not come to bring peace, but a sword," declares Jesus (Matthew 10:34). And the sword that he wields, the one that pierces Hazel Motes's sight and that of anyone else who will see it, is a sword of truth that sets the world on end. Into God's kingdom, as Jesus declares and O'Connor writes, "the lame shall enter first."[15]

Many Christian communities in the South and the ministers who serve them have lost the ability to embody a culturally challenging witness to the life-giving promises of Jesus Christ. As religion and literature scholar Ralph Wood points out, we "have lost what is repeatedly found in O'Connor's fiction: the glad news that God's goodness is even more shocking than our violations of it." Christian faith and ministry can no longer naturally be received through a Christian culture. Rather, it must be, Hazel Motes–like, "radically renewed in the church and perpetually given by God." We may not need to put out our own eyes to see this shattering truth, but we do need to find a way to see God rather than ourselves when we look through the window of faith.[16]

Ministers need not analyze too stringently this parabolic story to extract its message. Despite its rich biblical allusions and keen philosophical insight, the story plainly speaks of a Southern minister who cannot let loose of an overwhelming Jesus. If Hazel appears freakish to us, first in his denial of Christ and later in his sacrificial submission, it may be because today we have so shaped the Christian ministry to our own wants and needs that we cannot, dare not, face the likes of one who truly bears the mark of the cross upon his forehead. Ralph Wood claims, "The biblical plumbline reveals that the real deviant is not the shouting street preacher but the thoroughly well-adjusted man, the completely self-controlled woman, the utterly successful American." O'Connor is reputed to have altered John 8:32 by saying, "You shall know the truth, and the truth shall make you odd." And as Wood continues, "Christian faith produces literal eccentrics, people who are off-center because their lives have been made to circle about the real Center."

Motes is a misfit because Christian faith has made him so. His zeal shames us; his obsession with Christ frightens us. As one of my students who serves a small Methodist congregation in rural Arkansas commented after reading *Wise Blood*, "Shoot, if I was half as serious about proclaiming Jesus as Hazel is about denying him, my whole county would be on fire for the Lord." Though we'd rather not admit it, in a time when Christian ministry, especially in the Protestant mainstream, often settles for the same "practical heresies" of the rest of Western culture, Hazel Motes, the misfit minister, may just give us the jolt we need.[17]

Doing What He Tells Me to Do:
Taking Up Serpents in Lee Smith's *Saving Grace*

Reverend Virgil Shepherd, fifty-six-year-old pastor of the Jesus Name Church of God, located on Scrabble Creek outside Waynesville, North Carolina, in the 1950s, is dead set on what he believes. "I'm not running a scared race," he often claims. And "neither the threat of jail nor the fear of death could sway him," says Florida Grace, his teenage daughter and the story's narrator. Whether speaking in tongues, handling fire, or taking up deadly serpents in worship, Virgil Shepherd talks to God all the time. "You could hear him on the porch, or even out in the toilet," says Grace. He demands of his family a singular devotion to God. Their only book is the Bible; their only friends, those who attend his church. Virgil does these things, as Grace explains, "because Jesus required it of him."[18]

The creation of Grundy, Virginia, native Lee Smith, Virgil Shepherd is the real deal when it comes to mysticism. His congregation clearly accepts his Pentecostal mysticism; they actually thrive on it, experiencing through his leadership great outpourings of the Holy Spirit "in which the spirit of the Lord rested upon the brush arbor for an hour or more." But outside of the mountain congregations and communities, many see Virgil Shepherd as a misfit, out of step with contemporary culture. They label his Pentecostal fervor, glossolalia, and snake-handling rituals as "primitive." Sociologists explain the emotionalism of his congregational worship as "compensatory" for the economic hardships and social alienation of these isolated populations. Freudian psychologists might interpret the snake-handling rituals as pathological projection of "hysterically unacknowledged, and inadmissable desires." And the cultural elite frequently have great fun at the Pentecostal Holiness believer's expense. But along the mountain creeks and valleys of Tennessee, Virginia, Kentucky, North Carolina, and West Virginia, Virgil Shepherd, the mystic, is at home.[19]

His followers cannot resist Virgil's mysticism; his religious intensity magnetizes others. Grace explains:

> Once people met Daddy, they couldn't stay away. He was more alive than anybody else, with energy to spare, and in that poor place of hardscrabble farms and hand-to-mouth lives, he was the main thing happening. People were drawn to Daddy like bugs to a flame. He had something they wanted, and they'd stick around to find out what it was.

Whether in prayer, preaching and interpreting Scripture, healing the sick, handling snakes, or explaining his call, Virgil lights the fires of faith in those around him.[20]

The central sacrament of this rustic mystic is ritual enactment of the promises of Mark 16: "And these signs will accompany those who believe: by using my name they will cast out devils; they will speak in new tongues; they will pick up snakes in their hands, and if they drink any deadly thing, it will not hurt them; they will lay their hands on the sick, and they will recover" (Mark 16:17–18). Virgil's mysticism drives him to handle snakes and drink poison in order to reach a "new plateau" of faithfulness. He is prone to extended fasting, frequent glossolalia, and deep prayer. Some members of Virgil's congregation also display these "signs" of faith. Fannie, his wife, does not handle serpents, but she is anointed to handle hot coals without being burned. Virgil does not force such signs upon his family or members of the congregation. He knows that serpent handling is not given to everyone, only to the saints and in the form of an anointing.[21]

But when the time is right in certain worship services, maybe on Sundays after the preaching, or when a revival is going on, the mesmerizing Pentecostal ritual takes place. Virgil presides as chief mystic in these ecstatic moments of worship. He paces back and forth before the congregation as he preaches. As people begin to get "happy" in the Spirit, responding to the rhythmic yet simple music, leaping and shouting, dancing and clapping, the "anointing" comes upon the minister. "I can feel the power! Oh, I can feel the power right here tonight, Lord Jesus, oh thank you Lord, thank you, sweet Jesus!" Virgil exclaims. Then he opens up the box and takes out a snake and drapes it across his shoulder. The air goes "electric" as the Spirit empowers the mystic to take up the deepest, most biblical and archetypal symbol of evil and to handle it without fear of harm or death. The mystic's empowerment emboldens others to enter with him into this transcendent moment.[22]

Riveting as these signs are, something else is even more significant for Virgil's ministry: his voice. Virgil Shepherd's most powerful gift (charism) is his voice. The deep-seated Protestant reliance upon the spoken word as the means of divine revelation also holds true within Southern Christianity's Pentecostal and Holiness groups as God gathers the people around the word, revealed in Scripture and delivered through the voice of God's instrument, the minister, for the purpose of convicting sinners and imparting salvation. Virgil's voice invites response, as Grace describes.

> Even today, I don't know how to describe Daddy's voice, for that was surely one of his greatest blessings from the Lord. To start off with, he did not sound like a preacher. He did not fall into the singsong chant you hear so often. No, Daddy had a deep ringing voice and spoke real slow so that every word he said registered, and seemed to settle directly on the soul. He talked to God like he was sitting right across from Him, like they were old friends. He talked to everybody that same way, in fact, not like most preachers, who will yell at you and shame you and try to make you feel bad. Daddy's voice made you feel good, like you were strong in the Lord, and proud to do His will.

The voice builds up his hearers, makes them "strong in the Lord," and scatters "wonder and joy in the Jesus Name Church."[23]

Such is the spiritual power of Virgil Shepherd that even his long-suffering third wife, Fannie, sees him as a mystic and saint. His extended absences from home when he is out on preaching missions work an extreme hardship on Fannie and their four children. His extramarital affairs create conflict and shame. But none of this dissuades Fanny. As a reformed "dancing girl," she has been touched and saved by Virgil Shepherd's fire. She will not scorn him, no matter how extreme he becomes. "Your Daddy is a saint," Fannie would explain to the children, "a precious saint of God." Frequently shadows fall upon Fannie's face, but her love for Virgil is rooted in their intense spiritual connection and never fails. When the Spirit rains down upon Virgil Shepherd and the congregation, many will swear that he gives "off light like the sun." No one sees that light more brightly than Fannie.[24]

Readers will rightfully question Virgil Shepherd's domineering control of his wife and children. He is a strict disciplinarian and suspicious of all outside interference. His congregation is sectarian in its religious practices and its moral codes. The only book allowed in the house is the Bible. Social life is limited to those within their own congregation. When poisonous snakebites occur in worship, Virgil and his church members refuse medical treatment. By outside standards, these practices are abusive, oppressive of women and children, and in the case of snake handling, illegal and life threatening.

Yet ministers of the mainstream church should look closely, for Virgil reveals a mystical side that many mainstream Southern Christians never see. He makes a lasting contribution by establishing a congregation that sustains its members long after he departs. The spiritual fruits of patience, kindness, gentleness, forbearance, and compassion are evident in the lives of the members, even though they remember Virgil Shepherd's charismatic leadership with mixed emotions. Some even say that his years with them were "dark days." But in this fictional affirmation of ex opere operato, Virgil's spiritual contributions to the congregation are not undone by his immorality and excess.[25]

Virgil Shepherd and *Saving Grace* clearly show one truth about the ministry of the mystic: *the mystic transgresses*. Whether a snake-handling Pentecostal such as Virgil Shepherd, an enraptured visionary such as Teresa of Avila, or a Trappist monk like Thomas Merton, the mystic blurs the boundaries between the sacred and the profane, the pure and impure. The mystic's religious practices—prayer, sacred dance, song, trance, snake handling—are charged with a surplus of energy, often erotic, that the mystic directs toward God but that also spills over within the congregation. Through prayer and worship, the mystic receives and generates a magnetic force—the Holy Spirit—while moving dangerously close to the Holy Other that both threatens and purifies. Most of us feel far too vulnerable to drop the psychological, physical, and spiritual defenses with which we protect ourselves from the abyss. But in the presence of the mystic, for however a brief time, the Christian believer has a guide who can assist the seeker to dance, literally and figuratively, into the whirlwind of God and to come out transformed on the other side.

Many argue that we should guard against a mystic minister who is willing to put others in harm's way. No doubt many would distinguish the fiery enthusiasm of the Pentecostal Virgil Shepherd from the quiet contemplation of other mystics in the Christian tradition such as George Fox of the Quakers or the Roman Catholic Thomas Merton. After all, courting poisonous snakebite and drinking strychnine seems like a sure formula for an early appointment with death. And for this reason, most states have outlawed these practices. In such extreme actions there is a thin line between demonstrating one's faith and putting God to the test. Most of us would rather not try to figure out the difference.

But in other forms of mysticism—dancing in the Spirit, speaking in tongues, prophesying, contemplation—the mystic so frequently crosses over into the refining fire of the holy that he or she may or may not be aware of the peril this holds for others who are more dependent upon structure than spirit. By definition, the complete loss of self-consciousness that occurs in mystical experiences would make it impossible for the mystic to be fully responsible for the lives of others. As Saint Teresa of Avila explains, "The soul is fully awake as regards God, but wholly asleep as regards things of this world and in respect of herself."[26]

For this reason, the true minister as mystic, just as Virgil Shepherd in the novel, does not force others to follow; in fact, the mystic cautions others about the risks involved in abandoning oneself to God. The mystic minister pauses at the boundaries of the known world and reminds the follower that once one steps off the map, anything can happen. Trusting in the boundary-transgressing Christ—the one who says, "Those who want to save their life will lose it" (Mark 8:35)—the mystic will take others along for the journey, but only if they recognize, as Virgil Shepherd says, that "neither the fear of jail nor the threat of death will sway him."[27]

Given all this, the minister as mystic is a rare figure in mainline Southern religion, and there is almost no place there for his transgressive practices. Determined to keep God in a box, mainline white Protestants easily dismiss the mystic as an "oddball" or "quack." Pentecostal snake handlers like Virgil are an affront to the bland spiritual sensibilities of our modern culture and civic religion. But as writer Dennis Covington points out, snake handling didn't just start by itself in the mountains. "It started when people came down from the hills to discover they were surrounded by a hostile and spiritually dead culture." In the border communities between mountain and modern developments, places like Newport, Tennessee, and Sand Mountain, Alabama, these Bible believers threw up their defenses. "When their own resources failed, they called down the Holy Ghost. They put their hands through fire. They drank poison. They took up serpents."[28]

Obviously, ministers and laypersons do not *choose* to become mystics. Mystics are chosen by God. Many within the mainstream of Southern Protestantism are probably happy not to have been chosen for such intense spiritual lives. But Virgil Shepherd offers an intriguing invitation to those among the mainstream whose ministry seems moribund. On the outskirts of our towns and within the inner cities of our Southern metropolitan areas are ministers and congregations who believe that the holy erupts into Christian worship as tongues of fire and with ecstatic utterances. They are dead serious about serving this energizing God in worship and in daily life. We may not all elect to worship in their manner. It may frighten us too much, or it may not be the best expression of our own spiritual gifts.

But these Southern mystics invite us just the same to consider, Where are the "signs and wonders" in our own places of ministry? How is the Holy God being poured out upon the believers around us? And most important, what are the fruits of a Spirit-filled ministry for us? Is there any evidence in our ministries that the Holy God has been hanging around?

Bent Out of Shape for Christ's Sake

Hazel Motes and Virgil Shepherd send off exotic sparks of holy light that, whether they always intend it or not, ignite the faith of others and draw followers in closer to the flame of divinity.

As a mystic, Virgil Shepherd is a visionary whose hunger for ecstatic religious experience turns out to be a hunger shared by others. His dangerous rattlesnake rituals occur within public worship and thereby help bind other believers to one another and God. Though unique (and controversial), his mystical ministry is in the service of others. Theologian and ethicist Barbara Holmes would call him a "public mystic"; his mystical fanaticism actually builds up the Christian community that he serves.[29]

Significantly, both of these ministers are eccentrics, which is a large part of their literary appeal. Whether by choice or circumstance, they are both out of step with the wider culture. Within a calling that subtly yet inexorably presses its ministers toward social conformity, their oddity makes them holy fools whose unconventional wisdom strikes a note of authenticity. Their dislocation in relationship to mainstream culture may be their saving grace and their most significant contribution to all of us ministers. These misfit and mystic ministers signify within themselves how conformity to the cross and resurrection of Jesus Christ bends out of shape all who are willing to become "fools for Christ" (1 Corinthians 4:10). They are unlikely saints in the tradition of the ancestral shaman, the Christian monastic, and the Protestant holy man and woman—figures whose lives are partly shrouded in mystery yet bracingly clear when speaking to the community. They are ministers who have figuratively abandoned their automobiles, video screens, marketing strategies, and all other gimmicks and mechanisms that displace ministry with self-reliance and technological wizardry.

Marginalized themselves, these two ministers show us what it means to champion those kingdom people who are blessed in the Gospels—the poor, the meek, the hungry, and the reviled—but whom the institutional church rarely sees. By boldly pointing toward the love of Christ among these forgotten ones, they righteously transgress the walls of exclusion in the church. When called upon to act, they do not hide behind the professional caution that can hamstring the ministry. Rather, as Virgil Shepherd says, "I will do what the Lord tells me to do, I will go where He tells me to go."[30] Like Hazel Motes, mystics and misfits can swing the two-by-four of Christian truth hard enough to knock sense into the sleepy church and its ministers. "If you've been redeemed, I wouldn't want to be."[31]

Their eccentric spiritual journeys call into question our usually predictable approaches to ministry. To be sure, few of us will run out to take up serpents after meeting Virgil Shepherd, and hopefully none of us will imitate the self-immolation of Hazel Motes. But their extreme expressions of faith, emanating from the wild and windy place where Spirit kisses flesh and ignites human hearts into flame, can provide a bracing clarity to our own faith and ministry—a ministry that too often is devoid of mystery, too frequently staked to hollowed-out routine. Their genius and gift as fictional ministers is in showing us compelling images of the ministry and Southern religion that call us out of professional complacency and into the pulse and throb of authentic Christian faith and action.

10

Out in the Open

The Minister as Community Person

His wife had been dead twenty years, he had the reverential love and
respect of the whole countryside, but something was driving the man,
and, withal, there was often a species of amused cheerfulness about him
almost like elation, as though he were keeping some wonderful secret.
—Father Russell speaking of Rev. Tarmigian in Richard Bausch's "Design"

It doesn't take long for new ministers—one Sunday will usually do it—
to figure out that the ordained ministry is much bigger than themselves
and their own personal call from God. It is true that Protestants have
always stressed the personal, inward call of God as a moving force for
ordination. And many of the ministers discussed in these pages consider
their call as an inward response to God. But the church, as emphasized
by John Calvin, has also stressed that ordained ministry is in response
to an outward call. The Christian congregation summons the ordained
to minister "on behalf of" the community. Through ordination, the
minister becomes a "community person," no longer speaking for himself alone but also on behalf of the Christian congregation. In other
words, the minister is a representative Christian who in their office
stands for the community as a whole. As William Willimon puts it, the
minister is "under orders" to stand up for the community. Ministers
speak to God on behalf of the community, serve as host at community
meals, support the widow and orphan, visit those in prison, and bless
the community at births, baptisms, marriages, and deaths. Ministers do
not do these things by their own lights but by the power of God *and* the
authorization of the church.[1]

But despite this community responsibility, the minister does not
crowd out ministering to the laity. Rather, as community representative,
the ordained minister builds up the service of all other believers through
the ministry of preaching, serving at the table, and organizing the fel-

lowship. The minister is "under orders" and thus carries out the work with a sharp eye trained upon the whole body of Christ. Accepting the yoke of leadership, she becomes the symbolic community "character," bearing in herself the traits of the community that distinguish it as a Christian congregation. She reminds the congregation from week to week of who they are as human beings and who God calls them to be as sinners saved by grace. As Stanley Hauerwas puts it, "The clergy do what they do because what they do are activities that all Christians share in common."[2]

With the image of the minister as community person, we loop back around to the matter of vocation, where this study began. For without the calling of God *and* of the community, the minister does not have an official vocation. The ordained minister only knows herself as minister in relationship to those whom she represents. Failure to understand this fundamental fact of ordination bedevils many sincere Christians.

Many Southern writers only circle around the representative character of the ordained, swooping in on the minister's failure to adequately fulfill the role of community person. The problem may be that most people, including writers, perceive ministry in individualistic terms. Ministers are "characters" alright—and Southern fiction is chock full of them—but they are not community characters embedded within the larger theological and social world known biblically as the body of Christ. The individual minister functions more like a solitary God-seeker or religious entrepreneur—with all the accompanying distortions that arise from such characters—than as a symbol bearer for the community. In fiction, the lone-ranger minister can lead to colorful characters, but in real life, such a minister is far from complete.[3]

Happily, every now and then we do catch glimpses of what it looks like for the minister to be rooted within the community as a representative Christian. One minister from Southern fiction who helps to clarify our view of the minister as community person is Richard Bausch's Rev. Tarmigian.

Nothing out of the Ordinary:
The Art of Living and Dying in Richard Bausch's "Design"

At first glance, Richard Bausch's short story "Design" might appear to be an odd tale to use to shed light upon the role of the minister as community person, in large part because nothing much seems to happen.

Set in a small town in the Tidewater region of Virginia, the story is about the intersecting lives and habits of two ministers: Rev. Tarmigian, a seventy-two-year-old Baptist preacher with a chronic cough; and Father Russell, a forty-three-year-old Catholic priest with delicate sensibilities. They live within shouting distance of each other and, within the course of the story, visit each other on a regular basis. Their congregations only appear peripherally in the story, and we meet only a few members. It doesn't sound like a promising prospect for helping readers to discover the treasures of the minister as a representative of the community.

But small touches within the story suggest a much wider scope. The tightly woven exchanges between the priest and minister occur within the larger setting of their congregations and community. The community hovers on the edge of the story, reinforcing how the minister and the priest connect (or fail to connect) with the whole. For example, when Tarmigian refers to himself jokingly as "Reverend Fixture," we recognize a pastor who has served so long among a specific people, for more than three decades in his case, that he is a community "institution." And when we learn that Father Russell, who has just moved from New York to Virginia, views his parish assignment to the small Virginia township as the "accidental equivalent of a demotion," we hear a minister whose voice is out of sync with the community. Believing himself superior to the congregation, Russell is unable to care for them as their ordained representative. He looks upon the congregation as an outsider, whereas Rev. Tarmigian knows the community from the inside out.[4]

The story centers on the Catholic priest's attempts to understand himself and the ministry through his Protestant counterpart. The two are opposites, and their differences are clear: Tarmigian is elderly, widowed, humorous, and brims with physical energy, "raking leaves all morning in the fall breezes." Russell is barely middle-aged, never married, and sedate. Tarmigian is garrulous and extroverted, enjoying "the reverential love and respect of the whole countryside," whereas Russell is reticent and withdrawn. While Tarmigian dismisses his persistent, dry cough as a lingering summer cold, Russell is anxiety ridden that "every twist or turn of his body . . . signified the onset of disease." Though old and apparently sick, Tarmigian does not fear death; Russell, though young, is self-indulgently morbid, focusing on himself to the point of distraction. Tarmigian relishes engagement with his parishioners, such as the Aldenberrys who after fifty-two years of marriage want a divorce. He asks them, "I mean, when do you think the phrase 'sticking it out' would stop being applicable?" Father Russell, in contrast, disdains his parishioners. When saying the morning mass, he thinks, "The stolid, calm faces of his parishioners were almost ugly in their absurd confidence in him, their smiles of happy expectation and welcome." In the contrasting characters, we see the difference between a minister who serves as a community person and one who does not.[5]

Every day from his study window, the priest watches the older minister get on with his life and his ministry. Russell observes that he rakes the leaves with an "amused cheerfulness almost like elation." Tarmigian's easy lack of self-regard, especially about his own health, needles Russell, who frets and worries about his neighbor, but Tarmigian dismisses his concerns: "I'm fine. There's no need for anyone to worry."[6]

Tarmigian's manner and attitude disorient Russell because for him ministry has slowly devolved into excessive self-regard. Approaching vocational burnout, aware that he "might unconsciously be learning to use his vocation as form of refuge," the priest is more preoccupied with his own feelings and health than that of his parishioners. In contrast to Tarmigian, Russell observes that a "morbid anxiety about his health was worsening." His nights are restless, "yet each morning his dazed waking—from whatever fitful sleep the night had yielded him—was greeted with the pall of knowing that the aging pastor of the next-door church would be out in the open, performing some strenuous task." Father Russell's self-obsession becomes so great that he can no longer pray; saying the mass makes him feel miserable and exhausted. In short, Father Russell has become so self-absorbed that he relegates God and the community to the sidelines. When Russell tries to explain his growing morbidity to Tarmigian, the old pastor knowingly smiles and says, "You're a good man, but you're learning a tendency."[7]

Father Russell projects his own consuming anxiety upon the affable Rev. Tarmigian. But the wise pastor will not indulge the priest in his tendency. He will not support Russell's self-obsession, and he cheerfully sets aside his own health concerns. Instead, Tarmigian, the representative minister, continues going about ministry and life in the same constant way that he has for thirty years as pastor of Faith Baptist Church in fictional Port Royal County, Virginia. He studies for an hour a day in his book-lined office, rakes the leaves in front of the parsonage, paints the interior of the house, visits parishioners in the hospital, and counsels with the Aldenberrys. In a manner that seems to be second nature, Tarmigian practices his ministry "out in the open" among the community while trying to be a friend to the self-absorbed Russell.

Tarmigian embodies ministry in a way that Father Russell cannot imagine for himself. He sees up close and in full public view the life of a fellow servant of the gospel who by his lack of self-preoccupation radiates "some wonderful secret." The secret, suggested by the title of the story, is that Tarmigian ministers with confidence in the hidden "design" of God. The old Calvinist preacher has a much firmer grasp on the providential *and* sacramental nature of life than his young Catholic colleague. The created order is chockablock full of joy-making revelation that is best seen if not viewed too directly. Self-humor helps in discerning the tracings of God within creation. Tarmigian's ministry functions sacramentally for Russell and for the community, which hovers on the periphery of the story, because the presence of God shines through the old minister's flesh-and-blood incarnation of the gospel. When Russell and the other members of the community see and talk with Tarmigian, they catch a glimpse of God's mercy and grace, filtering through his smiles and words. Tarmigian surely is not God for the community, but in word and deed he does point toward the presence of God among them.[8]

Tarmigian's greatest gift to Father Russell and the community is the way he approaches death. By the end of the story, it is clear that the elderly minister is dying. But so are we all, his life suggests. Rather than cave in to his growing illness and approaching death, Tarmigian faces it with humor and courage. At the story's closing, we are told that "even in the pall of his decline, [he was] amused by something." When Russell asks Tarmigian how he is doing, and the old pastor admits to a feeling a "little under the weather," it dawns on Father Russell, "with the force of a physical blow, that the old man knew quite well that he was dying."[9]

By story's end, Father Russell is so worried about Tarmigian's physical health that he interrupts the minister's counseling session with Mrs. Aldenberry. Tarmigian takes the interruption in stride. "Now, let's get to the flattering part of all this—you walking over here getting yourself all wet because you're worried about me." So when Tarmigian, in plain view of Mrs. Aldenberry, invites Russell to "Shake hands. No, let's embrace. Let's give this poor woman an ecumenical thrill," it is too much for Father Russell. He collapses into the minister's arms, "breathing the odor of bay rum and talcum, and of something else, too, something indefinable and dark." He begins to sputter and tremble as the old minister holds him. He cannot stop blubbering. They are tears of gladness, relief.[10]

Tarmigian, the dying, lifelong servant of the gospel, embraces Father Russell, who is terrified of death. The embrace restores Russell. He, too, senses the hidden design of God that buoys Tarmigian's ministry:

> Father Russell had a moment of sensing that everything Tarmigian had done or said over the past year was somehow freighted with this one moment, and it took him a few seconds to recognize the implausibility of such a thing. No one could have planned it, or anticipated it: this one aimless gesture of humor—out of a habit of humorous gestures, and from a brave old man sick to death—that could feel so much like health, like the breath of new life.

True to form, when Russell begins to regain his composure after this moment of tearful resurrection, and the hard-of-hearing Mrs. Aldenberry asks, "What's going on here?" Tarmigian responds, "Why nothing out of the ordinary." Nothing out of the ordinary, indeed. Only living and dying among the people of God.[11]

As community person, Tarmigian offers to Russell and the community the finest of arts: the art of living and dying well. What more could the community want than to be able to know another human being who is capable of guiding us in the art of life and death? Rev. Tarmigian provides such direction not with his words but with his habits, his daily practices of Christian living. He shows to Father Russell and the congregation how Christians live and how Christians die. His practices are simple and sustaining: daily study, physical exercise, constancy, humor, compassion, and friendship. Through his openness and integrity, Tarmigian radiates an image of the ministry where the goodness of God shines through the cracks.[12]

In the end, Tarmigian gives to Russell and the community members their own vocation. He models for them a life "worthy of the gospel" (Philippians 1:27). As a public person, Tarmigian's life is like an open book. In his directness, his courage to live and die "unto the Lord," he shows all Christians, ordained and lay alike, the portrait of a Christian whose life is worthy of imitation. Tarmigan would not claim that his life is particularly worthy of imitation, which is precisely the point. He quietly, almost imperceptibly subsumes his own needs, his own ego, even his own dying unto Christ. The old minister, as community representative, gently shows to others what Paul writes to the Galatians: "It is not longer I who live, but it is Christ who lives in me" (Galatians 2:20).

For a Preacher His Whole Life
Is His Witness and His Sermon

Robert Morgan concludes his novel *This Rock*, set in the Southern Appalachians, with words that boil down the essentials of the role of the minister as community person:

> A preacher don't have to be perfect. Nobody in this world is perfect. A preacher only gives what he has, all of what he has. What a preacher is, and what a preacher does, is as important as what he says in the pulpit. And what he says to the grieved and to the afflicted and troubled in their minds, is as important as what he says at a revival meeting. For a preacher his whole life is his witness and his sermon.

Perfection is not required of the Christian minister as community person. But by virtue of ordination, the minister's daily life is on public display. This is so because the members of the congregation need an official representative whose life and words speak for both themselves and the gospel of Jesus Christ.[13]

The public nature of Christian ministry goes with the territory of ordination. Jesus admonishes his followers, "Let your light shine before others, so that that they may see your good works and give glory" to God (Matthew 5:16). And Paul, more than willing to be an example to others, boldly says to the Corinthians, "Be imitators of me, as I am of Christ" (1 Corinthians 11:1). Ordination challenges ministers to accept the responsibility to live their lives, as Tarmigan does, "out in the open," where others can learn the shape of Christian living. The Episcopalians and their renegade cousins, the Methodists, call it being a "wholesome example" of the gospel. This witness to the gospel—by modeling a well-lived life yoked to the life, death, and resurrection of Jesus Christ—is no small thing.

This responsibility certainly is burdensome at times, especially among congregations whose expectations are unrealistic. Nothing about ordination suggests that the representative role of Christian ministry is easy. Pitfalls abound. Some people project their own demanding perfectionism upon the minister, whom they then condemn for failing to measure up. The minister's community role often pumps stress into the family, which sometimes has tragic consequences. But as Gregory the Great instructed pastors in the sixth century, "Those who carry the vessels of the Lord are those who undertake, in reliance on their way of living, to draw the souls of their neighbors to the everlasting places." The challenge for ministers who are willing to stand among the people, as pastoral theologians Greg Jones and Kevin Armstrong suggest, is to close the gap between their own character and the "definitive exemplar, Jesus Christ."[14]

It isn't that the minister must be pure so that the church members get off the moral hook within their own lives (even though some laity may unconsciously think so). Rather, the congregation looks toward a minister who, in the words of Hippolytus of Rome, tries to "minister blamelessly by night and day" in order to lead the congregation to do the same. The minister will surely botch things just like everyone else. But her ordination means that the minister lives life within public view so that everyone else can see how Christians try to live and die unto the Lord. Barbara Brown Taylor puts it this way in her memoir, *Leaving Church*:

> As my beloved rector had told me in seminary, being ordained is not about serving God perfectly but about serving God visibly, allowing other people to learn whatever they can from watching you rise and fall. "You probably won't be much worse than other people," he said, "and you certainly won't be any better, but you will have to let people look at you. You will have to let them see you as you are."

By watching the minister, the community learns that, yes, we are all sinners saved by grace, and that as grace-saved sinners we have a Savior much greater than ourselves to worship and serve.[15]

Ministers who think that they can avoid the challenge to publicly bring honor to their office are always sadly mistaken. And frequently they bring great harm to themselves and others. As Beth Patillo's clergywoman says in *Heavens to Betsy*, "The strange reality of being a minister is that your life does become the business of your congregation. They have a stake in you. If you mess up, it reflects on them. Your errors hurt them." Conversely, when the minister brings integrity to the office, it shines a brighter light upon the congregation as a whole. Difficult as it is, by the grace of God through Jesus Christ, ministers must learn to inhabit their office as community person in a way that edifies the whole people of God.[16]

Ultimately, the downfall of clergy character is due to the failure to rely upon the grace of Jesus Christ. Morally confused and destructive ministers are usually cut off from the sources of their own calling: *the grace of God experienced within Christian community.* Ministers as much as laity can become isolated from grace-filled community, and when they do, they begin to function as individual religious operators. This leads to either grandiose behavior (minister as hero), emotional distancing from others (minister as unavailable), or debilitating loneliness (minister as needy dependent). All manner of clergy immorality stems from these conditions, from embezzlement to bedding down with vulnerable parishioners.

On the other hand, many ministers strive to remain connected to the grace of Jesus Christ; they attempt to selflessly lead the congregation into the fullness of God's reign (kingdom). For their efforts to be genuine community persons, these ministers are sometimes beloved and sometimes detested. Those congregations that have their eyes wide open may embrace the minister as community person. Congregations that prefer counterfeit community will frequently cast off a minister who seeks to bring life among them to a more complete expression of the reign of God. Such congregations confuse proximity with community, wanting the forms of religion without the intimacy of community and the cost of commitment. After all, Jesus Christ bids the community to live and die with him. Not every congregation wants to embrace a minister whose words and deeds proclaim that invitation. Church and community need ministers who understand that God calls us not beyond ourselves but more into ourselves, a people made and remade in the image of God, not simply Christ-haunted but Christ-loved and redeemed people.

In the wisdom of God and throughout the history of the church, the ones whom God calls together, the people of God, have needed leaders who at least attempt and sometimes even succeed in embodying both the longings of the community *and* the response of God. As the North Carolina writer Allan Gurganus sees it, "One way of looking at this [the ministry] is to imagine that at every moment in history, there's a search committee looking for a preacher. And what they want in a preacher is everything they want for themselves at this moment." The one who is willing to faithfully fulfill that call from the congregation *and* God, even at great personal costs, is the one whom the church calls to be a "parson": a representative person.[17]

Epilogue

We long to be allied with two things: with all the people who came
before us—tradition—and also with our hope, so we can transcend life.
The church is indeed often a failure, but we don't have anything better.
It isn't fair just to walk away from it."
　　　—Doris Betts in W. Dale Brown's *Of Fiction and Faith*

Writers and ministers share common ground. Fiction like faith sometimes ends in failure: characters don't stir the imagination, and stories
fail to bend to the quivering contours of life and death. Southern writers, like those of any other region, often fall short of the mark of literary artistry, just as Southern ministers, like ministers everywhere, miss
the mark of faithfulness in ministry. But even in failure, writers in service to the creative impulse, just as ministers in service to Jesus Christ,
cannot easily walk away from their calling, even when excellence
remains more a hope than a fulfillment.

It remains my hope that these varied depictions of the minister in
Southern fiction might illuminate, however fleetingly, the Christian
ministry throughout the South and beyond. In all of these stories, we
have discovered ministers who are as distinct as the writers who created
them. We have encountered more than a little sarcasm and criticism of
the ministry, just as we have seen some strikingly sensitive portrayals.
Whether the lives of these fictional ministers, the way that they inhabit
the offices of ministry, their struggles with faith and doubt, their character strengths and weaknesses, and their response to God and the communities that they serve—whether all these can be instructive in terms
of real ministry is finally up to us as readers.

As the South changes yet endures, so too does its fiction and its faith.
Amid the flux, the minister remains the most visible representative of
the varieties of religious experience that continue to flourish across the

"Christ-haunted" landscape that is the South. They fire the imaginations of the region's writers who creatively present them to us in multiple visions of the ministry. If we listen to them, the fictional ministers have a word for us. Maybe *Wise Blood*'s Hazel Motes's intense rejection of Christ finally becomes a witness to us of what it means to give everything we've got to the One who joined suffering humanity through death upon a cross. It is possible that when we find ourselves aimlessly drifting in the doldrums of ministry, the goosed-up visionary L. Ray Flowers from *Lunch at the Piccadilly* or the truth-telling Byron Egan from *Yonder Stands Your Orphan* can snatch us out of our spiritual lethargy and reinvigorate our ordained pulses by showing us something worth living for. Maybe the clay from the feet of John Pearson in *Jonah's Gourd Vine* can help us accept our own humanity but offer it up to God in humility. Perhaps the slick conventions of Rev. Roger Hagan in *The Convention* can challenge ministers to avoid becoming our own worst stereotype, and to strive for honesty before God and others, even if not played out quite so publicly as that of Joe Pike Moseley in *Dairy Queen Days* or as problematically as Joel King in *Plain Heathen Mischief.* Hopefully, the emotions and longings for purpose and self-identity of ministers' spouses and children like Dean Lynch in *The Sunday Wife* or Grace Shepherd in *Saving Grace* can help ministers become more sensitive to those with whom they establish family covenant and become more aware of how the calling to ordained ministry always affects the family. The priestly role of the minister within Southern society, seen in Margaret Bonner in *Evensong* and Father John in *Lancelot*, is often overshadowed by the more prevalent Protestant image of the minister as preacher, evangelist, or pastor, but perhaps these fictional Southern priests will stretch our pastoral imaginations to see new opportunities for ministry that are grounded in both Word *and* sacrament.

I hope that at least a few of these characters will continue to live with us—some as reminders of who we do not want to become, and some as invitations to grow in grace toward the fullness of the new creation offered by Jesus Christ. When ministers or laypersons experience doubt of self and calling, maybe *Dairy Queen*'s Joe Pike Moseley's words, "Yea, verily," will float into our minds and at least assure us that in our doubts we are not alone. Holy friendships do matter. When we want to lament and implore God for some kind of sign in the middle of trouble, perhaps we can hear the depth-sounding words of Rev. Tarmigian in "Design," saying that even in our dying, there is "nothing out of the ordinary." Or maybe in a quiet moment of reflection, while preparing a sermon, setting the Lord's Table, or after a particularly satisfying moment of pastoral counsel, we will hear Margaret Bonner say, "May the simple grace of daily obligations be with you."

In the end, if my attempt to cast light upon the offices of the ministry through the lens of Southern fiction has been inadequate, if my scope has sometimes been too narrow and my gauge too shallow to capture the colorful complexity of my topic, and if I have too often lapsed into a didacticism that neither benefits readers or the church nor honors the creativity of Southern writers—it is so despite my best intentions. To which I can only say, borrowing the words from one of Southern fiction's most perceptive writers, Doris Betts, "Sometimes to rest with a grin on the bedrock of Original Sin can be downright relaxing."[1]

Permissions

Excerpts from *The Convention* by Will Campbell. Copyright © 2007 by Will Campbell. Reprinted by permission of Mercer University Press.

Excerpts from "Design," pp. 292–95, 297–98, 302–6, used as chapter opener and within text from *The Stories of Richard Bausch* by Richard Bausch. Copyright © 2003 by Richard Bausch. Reprinted by permission of HarperCollins Publishers.

Excerpts from *Evensong* by Gail Godwin, copyright © 1999 by Gail Godwin. Reprinted by permission of Ballantine Books, a division of Random House, Inc., and by permission of John Hawkins and Associates, Inc.

Excerpts from *In My Father's House* by Ernest J. Gaines, copyright © 1978 by Ernest J. Gaines. Used by permission of Alfred A. Knopf, a division of Random House, Inc.

Excerpts from pp. 88–89, 111–12, 128–31, 141, 202, used as chapter opener and within text from *Jonah's Gourd Vine* by Zora Neale Hurston. Copyright © 1934 by Zora Neale Hurston; renewed © 1962 by John C. Hurston. Reprinted by permission of HarperCollins Publishers and by Little, Brown Book Group Ltd.

Excerpts from *Juneteenth: A Novel* by Ralph Ellison (New York: Random House, Inc., 1999), 137. Copyright © 1999 by Ralph Ellison. Reprinted by permission of Penguin Books Ltd., and by Random House, Inc.

Excerpts from *Lancelot* by Walker Percy. Copyright © 1977 by Walker Percy. Copyright renewed 2005 by Mary Bernice Townsend Percy. Reprinted by permission of Farrar, Straus, and Giroux, LLC and by permission of McIntosh and Otis, Inc.

Excerpts from *Lunch at the Piccadilly* by Clyde Edgerton. Copyright © 2003 by Clyde Edgerton. Reprinted by permission of Algonquin Books of Chapel Hill.

Excerpts from *A Place Called Wiregrass* by Michael Morris. Copyright © 2000 by Michael Morris. Reprinted by permission of the author.

Excerpts from *Plain Heathen Mischief* by Martin Clark, copyright © 2004 by Martin Clark. Used by permission of Alfred A. Knopf, a division of Random House, Inc.

Excerpt from "The River" in *A Good Man Is Hard to Find and Other Stories*, copyright © 1948, 1953, 1954, 1955 by Flannery O'Connor, © renewed in 1976 by Mrs. Edward F. O'Connor, and in 1981, 1983 by Regina O'Connor, reprinted by permission of the Mary Flannery O'Connor Charitable Trust via Harold Matson Co., Inc. and Harcourt, Inc.

Notes

Introduction

1. William Price Fox, *Southern Fried Plus Six* (Philadelphia: Lippencott, 1968).

2. Flannery O'Connor, *Mystery and Manners: Occasional Prose,* edited by Sally and Robert Fitzgerald (New York: Farrar, Straus & Giroux, 1993), 44.

3. Of the many who continue to claim that the religion of the South is still predominantly conservative and evangelical, see Charles Reagan Wilson, *Judgement and Grace in Dixie: Southern Faiths from Faulkner to Elvis* (Athens: University of Georgia Press, 1995), chap. 1; Charles Reagan Wilson and Mark Silk, eds., *Religion and Public Life in the South: In the Evangelical Mode,* Religion by Region Series (Walnut Creek, CA: AltaMira Press, 2005); John Boles, *The Great Revival: Beginnings of the Bible Belt* (Lexington: University Press of Kentucky, 1996); Samuel S. Hill, *Southern Churches in Crisis Revisited* (Tuscaloosa: University of Alabama Press, 1999).

4. This is the basic claim of Peter Applebome in *Dixie Rising: How the South Is Shaping American Values, Politics and Culture* (New York: Harcourt, Brace, 1996) and John Egerton in *The Americanization of Dixie: The Southernization of America* (New York: Harper's Magazine Press, 1974); see Fred Hobson, *Tell about the South: The Southern Rage to Explain* (Baton Rouge: LSU [Louisiana State University] Press, 1983), 16; John Egerton, *The Americanization of Dixie,* xix.

5. Louis D. Rubin, "The Historical Image of Modern Southern Writing," *Journal of Southern History* 22 (May 1956): 154–55.

6. James C. Cobb, *The Most Southern Place on Earth: The Mississippi Delta and the Roots of Regional Identity* (New York: Oxford University Press, 1992); Eudora Welty, "Sense of Place," in *The Eye of the Story: Selected Essays and Reviews* (New York: Random House, 1983), 128; Ralph Ellison, *Invisible Man* (New York: Vintage, 1995), 577, as cited in Betsy Fancher, "My Flannery O'Connor," *Brown's Guide to Georgia* 3 (1975): 16–22.

7. I have arbitrarily left out the writers from Texas, which helps limit my task, but the Southwest literature, especially that of Texas, is often considered part of Southern fiction. For a thoughtful overview of the contemporary debate of southernness in Southern literature, see Scott Romine, "Where Is Southern Literature? The Practice of Place," in *South to a New Place: Region, Literature, Culture,* ed. Suzanne W. Jones and Sharon Monteith (Baton Rouge: LSU Press, 2002). For a specific discussion of Mark Twain's Southernness, see Louis J. Budd, "Mark

Twain," in *The Companion to Southern Literature*, ed. Joseph M. Flora and Lucinda H. MacKethan (Baton Rouge: LSU Press, 2002), 917–18. See also Richard Gray, *Writing the South: Ideas of an American Region* (Cambridge: Cambridge University Press, 1986), 120–21; and Louis D. Rubin, *The Faraway Country: Writers of the Modern South* (Seattle: University of Washington Press, 1963), 4ff.

Chapter 1: Whose Voice Is That?

1. William H. Willimon, *Pastor: The Theology and Practice of Ordained Ministry* (Nashville: Abingdon, 2002), 18–19. See also E. Brooks Holifield, *God's Ambassadors: A History of the Christian Clergy in America* (Grand Rapids: Eerdmans, 2007).

2. Barbara Brown Taylor, *The Preaching Life* (Boston: Cowley, 1993), 26.

3. Charles Reagan Wilson, "Flashes of Spirit," *Image: A Journal of Arts and Religion* 24 (Fall 1999): 77; Doris Betts, "The Fingerprint of Style," in *Voicelust: Eight Contemporary Fiction Writers on Style*, ed. Allen Wier and Don Hendrie Jr. (Lincoln: University of Nebraska Press, 1985), 9.

4. Wendell Berry, *Jayber Crow* (Washington, DC: Counterpoint, 2000), 43.

5. Peggy Payne, *Revelation* (New York: Simon and Schuster, 1988), 12–13, 180, 74.

6. Hill, *Southern Churches in Crisis Revisited*, xvi.

7. Thomas G. Long, *The Witness of Preaching* (Louisville, KY: Westminster John Knox Press, 1990), 11.

8. Richard Wright, "Fire and Cloud," in *Uncle Tom's Children* (New York: Perennial, Harper Collins, 2004), 219.

9. H. L. Mencken, "The Sahara of the Bozart," in *Prejudices: Second Series* (New York: Knopf, 1920), 136–37; Clyde Edgerton, *Killer Diller* (New York: Ballantine, 1996), 167.

10. Sherri Holman, *The Mammoth Cheese* (New York: Atlantic Monthly Press), 238, 242, 143.

11. Ferrol Sams, *Whisper of the River* (New York: Penguin, 1986), 385.

12. Robert Inman, *Dairy Queen Days* (Boston: Little, Brown, 1997), 85.

13. Sandra Hollins Flowers, "Hope of Zion," in *The Christ-Haunted Landscape: Faith and Doubt in Southern Fiction*, Susan Ketchin (Jackson: University Press of Mississippi, 1994), 174–83.

14. Inman, *Dairy Queen Days*, 17, 8.

15. Ibid., 274–75.

16. Flowers, "Hope of Zion," 183.

17. Bobbie Ann Mason, "The Retreat," in *God: Stories*, ed. C. Michael Curtis (New York: Houghton Mifflin, 1998), 137.

18. *The Confessions of St. Augustine*, trans. F. J. Sheed, ed. Michael P. Foley (Kansas City, KS: Sheed, Andrews and McMeel, 1970), 146. See John Boles, *The Great Revival, 1787–1805: The Origins of the Southern Evangelical Mind* (Lexington: University Press of Kentucky, 1972); Christine Leigh Heyerman, *Southern*

Cross: The Beginnings of the Bible Belt (Chapel Hill: University of North Carolina Press, 1997).

19. Horton Davies, *A Mirror of the Ministry in Modern Novels* (New York: Oxford University Press, 1959), 51ff., chap. 3. Inman, *Dairy Queen Days,* 123; Payne, *Revelation,* 284.

20. From a personal conversation with the authors, October 2004; July 2004.

21. Allan Gurganus, "When I'm Fog on a Coffin Lid," in Ketchin, *The Christ-Haunted Landscape,* 391.

Chapter 2: Riding the Word

1. Ralph C. Wood, *Flannery O'Connor and the Christ-Haunted South* (Grand Rapids: Eerdmans, 2004), 177; Karl Barth, *Homiletics* (Grand Rapids: Eerdmans, 1991), 48–49.

2. See Harold Woodell, "Preaching," in Flora and MacKethan, *Companion to Southern Literature,* 680–82.

3. Ralph Ellison, *Juneteenth: A Novel,* ed. John F. Callahan (New York: Random House, 1999), 354; Lee Smith, *Saving Grace* (New York: G. P. Putnam's Sons, 1995), 17.

4. Lisa Alther, *Original Sins* (New York: Knopf, 1981), 246–47.

5. Frederick Buechner, *Wishful Thinking: A Theological ABC* (New York: Harper & Row, 1973), 87.

6. James Earl Massey, *The Burdensome Joy of Preaching* (Nashville: Abingdon, 1998); John Chrysostom, *On the Priesthood,* in *The Nicene and Post-Nicene Fathers,* ed. Philip Schaff, vol. 9 (Grand Rapids: Eerdmans, 1989), 70–71.

7. Ellison, *Juneteenth,* 137, 38, 41; Dolan Hubbard, *The Sermon and the African American Literary Tradition* (Columbia: University of Missouri Press, 1994), 72.

8. Barbara A. Holmes, *Joy Unspeakable* (Minneapolis: Fortress Press, 2004), 31.

9. Ellison, *Juneteenth,* 44. See Barbara A. Holmes, "Christ, Coltrane, and the Jazz Sermon: Preaching Love Supreme," *The African American Pulpit* 6 (Fall 2003).

10. Ellison, *Juneteenth,* 139.

11. Terry Kay, *The Year the Lights Came On* (Boston: Houghton Mifflin, 1976), 188.

12. Ibid.

13. Ibid., 189.

14. Ibid., 178.

15. Ibid., 189–90.

16. Ibid., 190.

17. On practicing Christian forgiveness, see Gregory L. Jones, *Embodying Forgiveness: A Theological Analysis* (Grand Rapids: Eerdmans, 1995).

18. Michael Morris, *A Place Called Wiregrass* (Tulsa, OK: River Oak Publishing, 2002), 186.

19. Ibid., 187.

20. Ibid., 209, 290–91; William Willimon, *Calling and Character: Virtues of the Ordained Life* (Nashville: Abingdon, 2000), 21. Willimon says, "By remaining disjoined from service to the text, and having no vocation to serve the Word, all I can do is serve the congregational status quo, run pastoral errands for the world as it is rather than let God use me to create a new world. And that is not only not fun, it's also immoral" (26).

21. Morris, *Wiregrass,* 31; John Calvin, *Institutes of the Christian Religion,* ed. John T. McNeill, Library of Christian Classics 20 (Philadelphia: Westminster Press, 1960), 1.14.1.

22. For a challenge to the Protestant mainline regarding blue-collar ministry, see Tex Sample, *Blue-Collar Ministry: Facing Economic and Social Realities of Working People* (Valley Forge, PA: Judson Press, 1984).

23. Morris, *Wiregrass,* 186–87.

24. Robert Olen Butler, "Up by Heart," in *Had a Good Time: Stories from American Postcards* (New York: Grove Press, 2004), 212.

25. Betts, "Fingerprint of Style," in *Voicelust,* 10; Martin Luther, *Sermons of Martin Luther: The Church Postils,* trans. John Lenker, vol. 1 (Grand Rapids: Baker, 1983, 1995), 44.

26. Willimon, *Pastor,* 66.

27. Flannery O'Connor, "The River," *Three by Flannery O'Connor* (New York: Signet, 1983), 152.

Chapter 3: You Didn't Even Count Before

1. H. L. Mencken's relentlessly satirical view of Southern Christianity cemented the stereotype of the manipulative evangelist in the broader North Amercian cultural imagination. For example, see his broadside of Tennessee hill country religion during the Scopes Trial era in "The Hills of Zion," in *Prejudices: Fifth Series* (New York: Knopf, 1926). For a brief summary of the history of the satiric depiction of the clergy in Southern fiction, see Charles Woodell, "Preaching," in *The Companion to Southern Literature: Themes, Genres, Places, People, Movements, and Motifs,* ed. Joseph M. Flora, Lucinda H. MacKethan, and Todd W. Taylor (Baton Rouge: Louisiana State University Press, 1991), 680–83.

2. For a trenchant analysis of the individualism that has hampered Southern religion, see James McBride Dabbs, *Who Speaks for the South?* (New York: Funk & Wagnalls, 1964), 113, 281ff.; O'Connor, *Mystery and Manners,* 34.

3. O'Connor, "The River," 31.

4. Ibid., 40.

5. Ibid., 40–41.

6. Ibid., 44–45.

7. Ibid., 48.

8. Ibid., 51–52.

9. O'Connor, *Mystery and Manners,* 162.

10. Barry Hannah, *Yonder Stands Your Orphan* (New York: Grove Press, 2001), 11.

11. Ibid.

12. Ibid., 9, 49, 71–72.

13. Ibid., 12; see Walter Wink, *Unmasking the Powers* (Philadelphia: Fortress Press, 1986).

14. Hannah, *Yonder Stands Your Orphan*, 232.

15. Ibid., 309, 283; Barry Hannah, "Christ in the Room," *Oxford American* 48 (Winter 2005): 74–75.

16. Hannah, *Yonder Stands Your Orphan,* 310.

17. Hannah, "Christ in the Room," 74–75.

18. John Chrysostom, *Homilies on Ephesians,* Hom X, in *A Select Library of the Nicene and Post-Nicene Fathers of the Christian Church,* ed. H. Wace and P. Schaff, Series 1, vol. 13 (New York: Christian Literature Co., 1887–1900), 100–101.

19. Applebome, *Dixie Rising,* 20.

20. Hannah, *Yonder Stands Your Orphan,* 297, 229.

21. For a pastoral theological study of the overlapping offices of the minister, see Thomas Oden, *Pastoral Theology: Essentials of Ministry* (San Francisco: Harper & Row, 1982); and G. Lee Ramsey Jr., *Care-full Preaching* (St. Louis: Chalice Press, 2002). Hannah, "Christ in the Room," 73.

Chapter 4: Pour Out Your Hearts

1. Richard Lischer, *Open Secrets: A Memoir of Faith and Discovery* (New York: Broadway, 2002), 50.

2. Hauerwas cited from Willimon, *Pastor,* 60; see Eugene H. Peterson and Marva J. Dawn, *The Unnecessary Pastor: Rediscovering the Call* (Grand Rapids: Eerdmans, 2002), 2. On the shift from soul care to self-therapy, see E. Brooks Holifield, *A History of Pastoral Care in America: From Salvation to Self-Realization* (Nashville: Abingdon, 1983). Flannery O'Connor, *Wise Blood,* 2nd ed. (New York: Farrar, Straus & Giroux, 1962), author's note.

3. William Hoffman, "The Question of Rain," in *By Land, By Sea* (Baton Rouge: LSU Press, 1988), 160–61, 163.

4. Ibid., 161–62.

5. Ibid., 166, 172.

6. Ibid., 170.

7. Ibid., 171.

8. Ibid., 170–71.

9. Ibid., 172.

10. Ibid., 172–73.

11. Ibid., 174.

12. See Susan Gilbert, "Anne Tyler," in *Southern Women Writers: The New Generation,* ed. Tonette Bond Inge (Tuscaloosa: University of Alabama Press, 1990), 274.

13. Anne Tyler, *Saint Maybe* (New York: Knopf, 1991), 4.

14. Ibid., 3–4.

15. Ibid., 82–83, 102.

16. Ibid., 115–17.

17. Ibid., 119–20.

18. Elaine Ramshaw, *Ritual and Pastoral Care* (Philadelphia: Augsburg Fortress, 1987), 22.

19. Tyler, *Saint Maybe,* 120.

20. Ibid., 120–21.

21. Ibid., 121–22.

22. Ibid., 123–24, 121.

23. Ibid., 123. On the absence of a genuine language of sin in North American Christianity, see Marsha Grace Whitten, *All Is Forgiven: The Secular Message in American Protestantism* (Princeton, NJ: Princeton University Press, 1993).

24. Tyler, *Saint Maybe,* 107.

25. Ibid., 186, 213.

26. Ibid., 225.

27. Ibid., 225, 337.

28. Personal interview with Clyde Edgerton, September 9, 2004.

29. Doris Betts, *Souls Raised from the Dead* (New York: Knopf, 1994), 177.

30. Willimon, *Pastor,* 79; Phillips Brooks, *Lectures on Preaching* (New York: E. P. Dutton, 1877), 77.

Chapter 5: Lift Up Your Hearts

1. Conroy in Danny Romine Powell, *Parting the Curtains: Interviews with Southern Writers* (Winston Salem, NC: J. F. Blair, 1994), 80; Samuel S. Hill, ed., *Religion in the Southern States: A Historical Study* (Macon, GA: Mercer University Press, 1983), 403.

2. Recent studies number Catholics at 8 to 12 percent of the Southern population, including the high-density Catholic populations of Texas, Louisiana, Florida, and Maryland. Compared to the 70 to 75 percent of the Southern population who identify as broadly "Protestant," the contrast is striking. For some of the latest research see http://www.frinstitute.org/southern.htm and http://www.thearda.com; Wilson and Silk, *Religion and Public Life in the South.*

3. Clyde Edgerton, *Raney* (New York: Ballantine Books, 1985), 69.

4. Martin Luther, *The Babylonian Captivity*, in *Works of Martin Luther*, vol. 2 (Philadelphia: Muhlenberg Press, 1943), 279.

5. Walker Percy, *Lancelot* (New York: Avon Books, 1978), 29, 25, 11–12.

6. Ibid., 236; John F. Desmond, *Walker Percy's Search for Community* (Athens: University of Georgia Press, 2004), 147.

7. Percy, *Lancelot,* 7, 3–4. The therapeutic concept of the "good enough mother" comes from D. W. Winnicott's object relations theory, as in his *Playing and Reality* (New York: Basic Books, 1971). Therapist as "container" appears in

Melanie Klein, "Notes on Some Schizoid Mechanisms," in *Envy and Gratitude, and Other Works: 1946–1963* (New York: Dell, 1977).

8. Percy, *Lancelot,* 9.

9. Anton T. Boisen, *The Exploration of the Inner World: A Study of Mental Disorder and Religious Experience* (Chicago: Willett, Clark, 1936).

10. Percy, *Lancelot,* 7.

11. Ibid., 41; Percy, *The Message in the Bottle* (New York: Farrar, Straus & Giroux, 1975), 148.

12. Percy, *Lancelot,* 214; see Desmond, *Walker Percy's Search,* 147; Henri Nouwen, *The Living Reminder: Service and Prayer in Memory of Jesus Christ* (New York: Seabury Press, 1977).

13. Percy, *Lancelot,* 167, 173.

14. Ibid., 277.

15. Ibid., 278–79.

16. John Calvin, "Catechism of the Church of Geneva," in *John Calvin: Selections from His Writings,* ed. John Dillenberger (Missoula, MT: Scholars Press, 1975), 253.

17. Gail Godwin, *Evensong* (New York: Ballantine, 1991), 13.

18. Ibid., 9, 13.

19. Ibid., 18.

20. Ibid., 20.

21. See Barbara Brown Zikmund, Adair T. Lummis, and Patricia Mei Yin Chang, *Clergy Women: An Uphill Calling* (Louisville, KY: Westminster John Knox Press, 1998), chap. 3.

22. Ibid., 212, 11.

23. Ibid., 12.

24. Ibid., 32.

25. Godwin, *Evensong,* 121, 125–27.

26. Ibid., 394–95.

27. Current statistics show that women comprise 36 percent of all students entering accredited Protestant seminaries, up from 19 percent in 1978. Nationally, approximately 10 percent of all ordained clergy are women. For ordination statistics, see Barbara Brown Zikmund et al., *Clergy Women.*

28. With the exception of Erskine Caldwell's Sister Bessie in *Tobacco Road* (New York: C. Scribner's Sons, 1932) and the recently developed Reverend Betsy Blessing in Beth Patillo's *Heavens to Betsy* (Colorado Springs: Waterbrook, 2005), Rev. Margaret Bonner occupies a unique place in Southern literature. For novels set outside the South that feature female ministers, see Rachel Basch, *The Passion of Reverend Nash* (New York: W. W. Norton, 2003); Julia Spencer Fleming's mystery series that begins with *In the Bleak Midwinter* (New York: Thomas Dunne, 2002); and Christina Summers, *Thieves Break In* (New York: Bantam, 2004).

29. Godwin, *Evensong,* 127.

30. Peter Taylor, "The Decline and Fall of the Episcopal Church (in the Year of

our Lord 1952)," in *The Oracle at Stoneleigh Court* (New York: Ballantine, 1993), 239, 264.

Chapter 6: Lying and Conniving and Claiming It as Heaven Sent

1. Mencken, "Sahara of the Bozart," 136–37.

2. Richard Lischer, *The End of Words: The Language of Reconciliation in a Culture of Violence* (Grand Rapids: Eerdmans, 2005), 44.

3. For a case study account of clergy sexual abuse, see Marie M. Fortune, *Is Nothing Sacred? The Story of a Pastor, The Women He Sexually Abused, and the Congregation He Nearly Destroyed* (Cleveland: United Church Press, 1999). Gregory the Great, *Regula Pastoralis,* trans. and annotated by Henry Davis, SJ, *Ancient Christian Writers,* ed. Johannes Quasten and Joseph C. Plumpe, vol. 11, part I.2 (New York: Newman Press, 1978), 24.

4. Zora Neale Hurston, *Jonah's Gourd Vine* (New York: Perennial / Harper & Row, 1990), 89.

5. Ibid., 111–12.

6. Ibid., 88, 111.

7. Ibid., 128–29, 111.

8. Ibid., 129–31.

9. Ibid., 136.

10. See Linda H. Hollies, *Sister, Save Yourself! Direct Talk about Domestic Violence* (Cleveland: Pilgrim Press, 2006). For a contemporary fictional story of domestic violence, see Anna Quindlen's *Black and Blue* (New York: Delta Books, 1998).

11. Hurston, *Jonah's Gourd Vine,* 141.

12. Ibid., 202.

13. On the Tennessee case, see the *Memphis Commercial Appeal,* April 20, 2007, "Mary Winkler Convicted—3–6 Years." See Carol Adams and Marie Fortune, *Violence against Women and Children: A Christian Theological Sourcebook* (New York: Continuum, 1996).

14. For dealing with such violations, see Marie Fortune, *Keeping the Faith: Guidance for Christian Women Facing Abuse* (San Francisco: HarperSanFrancisco, 1995); Hurston, *Jonah's Gourd Vine,* 131.

15. Willimon, *Calling and Character,* 46–47; see Nancy Richards and Marie Fortune, *Heal and Forgive: Forgiveness in the Face of Abuse* (Nevada City, CA: Blue Dolphin, 2005); Marie Fortune, *Is Nothing Sacred: When Sex Invades the Pastoral Relationship* (San Francisco: Harper & Row, 1992).

16. See Sondra Ely Wheeler, "Virtue Ethics and the Sexual Formation of Clergy," in *Practice What You Preach: Virtues, Ethics, and Power in the Lives of Pastoral Ministers and Their Congregations,* ed. James F. Keenan, SJ, and Joseph Kotva Jr. (Franklin, WI: Sheed & Ward, 1999), chap. 5; Augustine as cited in Willimon, *Calling and Character,* 36.

17. See J. Fred Lehr, *Clergy Burnout: Recovering from the 70–Hour Work Week—and Other Self-Defeating Practices* (Minneapolis: Fortress Press, 2006). For a theological discussion of excellence in ministerial character, see L. Gregory Jones and Kevin R. Armstrong, *Resurrecting Excellence: Shaping Faithful Christian Ministry* (Grand Rapids: Eerdmans, 2006).

18. Martin Clark, *Plain Heathen Mischief* (New York: Knopf, 2004), 10.

19. Ibid., 379.

20. Ibid., 212.

21. Ibid., 212, 307.

22. Ibid., 308.

23. Ibid., 335, 315.

24. Ibid., 308–9.

25. Ibid., 142, 308.

26. Ibid., 387, 394.

27. Ibid., 393.

28. "Toward grace," from David Bottoms, "In a U-Haul North of Damascus," in *Armored Hearts: Selected and New Poems* (Port Townsend, WA: Copper Canyon Press, 1995), 29; Clark, *Plain Heathen Mischief*, 396.

29. Clark, *Plain Heathen Mischief*, 395.

30. Merton as cited in Paul Elie, *The Life You Save May Be Your Own: An American Pilgrimage* (New York: Farrar, Straus & Giroux, 2003), 264.

31. Clark, *Plain Heathen Mischief*, 395.

Chapter 7: A Good Church Slogan Is Hard to Come By

1. Carlyle Marney, *Priests to Each Other* (Valley Forge, PA: Judson, 1978), 10.

2. Robert Morgan, *This Rock: A Novel* (Chapel Hill, NC: Algonquin Books, 2001), 299.

3. For a particularly scathing treatment of ecclesiastical politics within the United Methodist Church, see Gregory Wilson, *The Stained Glass Jungle* (Garden City, NY: Doubleday, 1962), 21. I am grateful to Joseph Reiff for supplying details regarding this publication. A precursor to the above is Harold Frederic's *The Damnation of Theron Ware* (Chicago: Stone & Kimball, 1896).

4. See Thomas L. Connelly, *Will Campbell and the Soul of the South* (New York: Continuum, 1982), 37; Marshall Frady, *Southerners: A Journalist's Odyssey* (New York: New American Library, 1980), 377–78.

5. Will Campbell, *The Convention: A Parable* (Atlanta: Peachtree Publishers, 1988), 123, 186–87.

6. Ibid., 50, 65.

7. David Dark, *The Gospel according to America: A Meditation on a God-blessed, Christ-Haunted Idea* (Louisville, KY: Westminster John Knox Press, 2005), 62.

8. Campbell, *The Convention*, 231.

9. Ibid., 192.

10. Ibid., 396–97, 403.

11. Dark, *Gospel according to America*, 152.

12. Personal interview, October 9, 2004. See http://www.cassandrakingconroy .com/the_sunday_wife_story.htm; and http://www.southernscribe.com/reviews/ general_fiction/sunday_wife.htm.

13. See http://www.southernscribe.com/reviews/general_fiction/sunday_wife .htm.

14. Cassandra King, *The Sunday Wife* (New York: Hyperion, 2002) 7.

15. Ibid.; http://www.cassandrakingconroy.com/tsw/the_sunday_wife_story.htm.

16. King, *The Sunday Wife,* 5–6.

17. Ibid., 7.

18. Ibid., 11.

19. Ibid., 47, 318–19.

20. Ibid., 18, 67.

21. Ibid., 318.

22. Ibid., 318, 371.

23. Eugene Peterson, *Under the Unpredictable Plant: An Exploration in Vocational Holiness* (Grand Rapids: Eerdmans, 1994), 4. Ecclesiastical ambition fueled by corporate promotion mechanisms runs counter to Methodism's original understanding of clergy mission and deployment. See Thomas E. Frank, *Polity, Practice, and Mission of the United Methodist Church* (Nashville: Abingdon, 2006).

24. For a theology of ministry grounded in the cruciform excellence of Christ, see L. Gregory Jones and Kevin R. Armstrong's *Resurrecting Excellence: Shaping Faithful Christian Ministry* (Grand Rapids: Eerdmans, 2006).

25. King, *The Sunday Wife,* 384.

26. Doris Betts, "Mr. Shawn and Father Scott," in *The Gentle Insurrecton and Other Stories* (Baton Rouge: LSU Press, 1982), 58, 67.

27. H. Richard Niebuhr, with Daniel Day Williams and James Gustafson, *The Purpose of the Church and Its Ministry: Reflections on the Aims of Theological Education* (New York: Harper, 1956).

28. Flannery O'Connor, *The Violent Bear It Away,* in *3 by Flannery O'Connor* (New York: New American [1955] 1960), 447.

Chapter 8: Burning Coals upon Their Lips

1. Hurston, *Jonah's Gourd Vine,* 99.

2. For an attempt to balance the prophetic and pastoral in preaching, see G. Lee Ramsey Jr., *Care-full Preaching: From Sermon to Caring Community* (St. Louis: Chalice, 2000).

3. See John Egerton, *A Mind to Stay Here: Profiles from the South* (New York: Macmillan, 1970); "Demonstration plot for the Kingdom of God," Koinonia Farms Web site, http://www.koinoniapartners.org/index.html; Samuel S. Hill, *Southern Churches in Crisis Revisited* (Tusacaloosa: University of Alabama Press, 1999), xxiii.

4. Robert Michael Franklin, "Clergy and Politics: The Black Experience," in *Clergy Ethics in a Changing Society: Mapping the Terrain,* ed. James P. Wind et al. (Louisville, KY: Westminster/John Knox Press, 1991), 276. For a recent appraisal of Martin Luther King Jr.'s influence on church and society, see Lewis V. Baldwin, Rufus Burrow Jr., Barbara A. Holmes, and Susan Winfield Holmes, *The Legacy of Martin Luther King, Jr.: The Boundaries of Law, Politics, and Religion* (Notre Dame, IN: University of Notre Dame Press, 2002).

5. Walter Brueggemann, *The Prophetic Imagination* (Philadelphia: Fortress Press, 1978).

6. See William E. Montgomery, "Semi-Involuntary: African-American Religion," in Wilson and Silk, *Religion and Public Life in the South*, 79ff.; and Franklin, "Clergy and Politics," 284. In Franklin's typology of the varieties of activism within the black church, apparently Rev. Martin Luther King Sr. would be more of a progressive accommodationist and Martin Luther King Jr. a prophetic radical.

7. Martin Luther King Jr., "Letter from a Birmingham Jail," in *Why We Can't Wait* (New York: Harper & Row, 1964), 90, 92.

8. Cited in John Edgerton, *Speak Now against the Day: The Generation before the Civil Rights Movement in the South* (Chapel Hill: University of North Carolina Press, 1995).

9. Ernest Gaines, *In My Father's House* (New York: Vintage, 1992), 10.

10. Ibid., 10, 35.

11. Ibid., 166.

12. Ibid., 99.

13. Ibid., 102, 87.

14. Ibid., 92.

15. Public curiousity regarding the flaws of the prophetic leader is a subtext in the ongoing interest in the life of Martin Luther King Jr. See the concluding volume to Taylor Branch's three-volume biography of Martin Luther King Jr. and the civil rights movement, *At Canaan's Edge: America in the King Years, 1965–68* (New York: Simon & Schuster, 2006).

16. Gaines, *In My Father's House*, 136.

17. Ibid., 203, 214.

18. Ibid., 210–13.

19. Ibid., 214.

20. Notable exceptions—such as Reynolds Price's *The Good Priest's Son: A Novel* (New York: Scribner, 2005), Randall Keenan's *A Visitation of Sprits: A Novel* (New York: Grove Press, 1989), or Madison Smart Bell's *A Solidier's Joy* (New York: Ticknor & Fields, 1989)—quietly wade into the swirling currents of race and religion in the contemporary South, but few others seem called to the water's edge.

21. Linda Wagner-Martin, "The South as Universe," in *South to the Future: An American Region in the Twenty-first Century*, ed. Fred Hobson (Athens: University of Georgia Press, 2002), 46.

22. On religious diversity in the South, see Charles H. Lippy, "Diversity,

Religious," in *The New Encyclopedia of Southern Culture,* vol. 1, *Religion,* ed. Samuel S. Hill (Chapel Hill: University of North Carolina Press, 2006), 58.

23. Paul Harvey, "Social Activism," in *New Encyclopedia of Southern Culture,* 1:142.

24. Jonathan Franzen, "Perchance to Dream: In the Age of Images, A Reason to Write Novels," *Harper's Magazine* 292, no. 1751 (April 1996): 35–54.

25. Clyde Edgerton, *Lunch at the Piccadilly* (Chapel Hill, NC: Algonquin Books, 2003), 20, 82.

26. Ibid., 201.

27. Willimon, *Pastor,* 255; C. Edgerton, *Lunch at the Piccadilly,* 80–82.

28. C. Edgerton, *Lunch at the Piccadilly,* 62.

29. Clyde Edgerton, *Lunch at the Piccadilly: A Reader's Guide* (New York: Ballantine Books, 2004), 261.

30. Willimon, *Pastor,* 258.

31. Walker Percy, *Signposts in a Strange Land* (Farrar, Straus & Giroux, 1991), 320, 325.

32. Willimon, *Pastor,* 267.

Chapter 9: Signs Will Follow Them That Believe

1. Flannery O'Connor, *Mystery and Manners,* selected and edited by Sally and Robert Fitzgerald (New York: Noonday Press, Farrar, Straus & Giroux, 1993), 207; Flannery O'Connor, *Wise Blood* (New York: Farrar, Straus & Giroux, 1990), 32.

2. Ibid., 44.

3. Evelyn Underhill, *The Mystics of the Church* (New York: Schocken Books, 1964), 9.

4. William James, *The Varieties of Religious Experience,* Modern Library, new edition (New York: Random House, 1994), 457.

5. Smith, *Saving Grace,* 8.

6. O'Connor, *Wise Blood,* 20, 22.

7. Ibid., 22.

8. Ibid., 24.

9. Ibid., 10, 14.

10. O'Connor, *Mystery and Manners,* 45, 115; O'Connor, *Wise Blood,* 54.

11. O'Connor, *Wise Blood,* 105–6.

12. Ralph Wood, "Grits and Grace: Flannery O'Connor's Strange Alliance with Southern Fundamentalists," *Mars Hill Review* 13 (Winter/Spring 1999): 42, quoting Kallistos Ware from John Desmond, *Risen Sons: Flannery O'Connor's Vision of History* (Athens: University of Georgia Press, 1987), 15; O'Connor, *Wise Blood,* 214, 232, 222.

13. O'Connor, *Mystery and Manners,* 114–15.

14. O'Connor, *Wise Blood,* 113, author's note to the second edition; O'Connor, *Mystery and Manners,* 35.

15. O'Connor, "The Lame Shall Enter First," in *The Complete Stories* (New York: Farrar, Straus & Giroux, 1986), 445ff.

16. Wood, *Flannery O'Connor and the Christ-Haunted South*, 219–20, 9.

17. Ibid., 160.

18. Smith, *Saving Grace*, 18, 24.

19. Ibid., 22; for psychological analysis of snake handling, see Thomas G. Burton, *Serpent-Handling Believers* (Knoxville: University of Tennessee Press, 1993), 126ff.

20. Smith, *Saving Grace*, 16.

21. About snake handling, Birckhead in Burton, *Serpent-Handling Believers*, 179, says "to place serpent-handling into its larger theological contexts . . . It is not viewed as isloated, aberrant, or bizarre, but rather as an outgrowth of a long-standing religious emphasis. . . . One can leave a service or a home [of the snake handlers] and feel completely awed by the faith, sincerity, and mysterious power manifested by these people—sensing that somehow they know, feel, have something in their lives that is redeeming amidst a lost world."

22. Smith, *Saving Grace*, 20.

23. Ibid., 17, 34; For a thorough discussion on the understanding of language and preaching within the holiness traditions, see Jeff Todd Titon's *Powerhouse for God: Speech, Chant, and Song in an Appalachian Baptist Church* (Austin: University of Texas Press, 1988), esp. chaps. 4 and 7.

24. Smith, *Saving Grace*, 13, 21.

25. When asked if Virgil's gaping character flaws invalidate his ministry, the author, Lee Smith, energetically responds, "No. Not at all" (personal interview, February 24, 2006).

26. Teresa of Avila, as cited in William James, *The Varieties of Religious Experience* (London: Routledge, 2002), 316.

27. Smith, *Saving Grace*, 18.

28. Dennis Covington, *Salvation on Sand Mountain: Snake Handling and Redemption in Southern Appalachia* (New York: Penguin, 1996), xvii–xviii.

29. Barbara A. Holmes, *Joy Unspeakable: Contemplative Practices of the Black Church* (Minneapolis: Augsburg Fortress, 2004).

30. Smith, *Saving Grace*, 8.

31. Ibid.; O'Connor, *Wise Blood*, 16.

Chapter 10: Out in the Open

1. John Calvin, *Institutes of the Christian Religion*, ed. John T. McNeill, Library of Christian Classics 21 (Philadelphia: Westminster Press, 1960), 4.3.1053–68.

2. Stanley Hauerwas, *Christian Existence Today: Essays on Church, World, and Living in Between* (Grand Rapids: Brazos Press, 2001), 136.

3. As religious historian James Wind has observed, ministers in North American literature by and large operate as lone rangers, with neither the resources nor

the theological expectations of the congregation to orient them: "Never do we see the church or any other institution serve as a communal resource for these troubled loners" ("Ethics in America," in James Wind et al., *Clergy Ethics in a Changing Society*, 112).

4. Richard Bausch, "Design," in *The Stories of Richard Bausch* (New York: HarperCollins, 2003), 292, 295.

5. Ibid., 293, 297–98, 303.

6. Ibid., 293–94.

7. Ibid., 302, 298.

8. Ibid., 293.

9. Ibid., 303–4.

10. Ibid., 304–5.

11. Ibid., 305–6.

12. See Amy Plantinga Pauw, "Dying Well," in *Practicing Our Faith*, ed. Dorothy C. Bass (San Francisco: Jossey Bass, 1997), chap. 12.

13. Morgan, *This Rock*, 302.

14. Gregory the Great, *Pastoral Care,* trans. Henry Davis, SJ (New York: Newman Press, 1950), 2.2, p. 46, as cited in Jones and Armstrong, *Resurrecting Excellence*, 80, 86.

15. Hippolytus, as cited in Willimon, *Pastor*, 31; Barbara Brown Taylor, *Leaving Church: A Memoir of Faith* (San Francisco: Harper, 2006), 37.

16. Patillo, *Heavens to Betsy*, 20.

17. Gurganus, in Ketchin, *Christ-Haunted Landscape*, 393.

Epilogue

1. Betts, "Fingerprint of Style," in *Voicelust*, 22.

Selected Bibliography

Agee, James. *A Death in the Family*. New York: Vintage, 1998.

Alter, Lisa. *Original Sins*. New York: Plume, 1996.

Baldwin, James. *Go Tell It on the Mountain*. New York: Dial Press, 1963.

Bausch, Richard. "Design." In *God: Stories*. Edited by C. Michael Curtis. Boston: Houghton Mifflin, 1998.

———. *Real Presence*. Baton Rouge: Louisiana State University Press, 1999.

———. *Thanksgiving Night*. New York: HarperCollins, 2006.

Bell, Madison Smartt. *Soldier's Joy*. New York: Ticknor & Fields, 1989.

Berry, Wendell. *Jayber Crow*. Washington, DC: Counterpoint, 2000.

Betts, Doris. "Family Album" and "Mr. Shawn and Father Scott." In *The Gentle Insurrection and Other Stories*. Baton Rouge: Louisiana State University Press, 1982.

———. *Souls Raised from the Dead*. New York: Knopf, 1994.

Brown, Mary Ward. "A New Life." In *The Christ-Haunted Landscape: Faith and Doubt in Southern Fiction*. Compiled by Susan Ketchin. Jackson: University Press of Mississippi, 1994.

———. "Tongues of Flame." In *Tongues of Flame*. New York: E. P. Dutton, 1986.

Brown, Larry. "A Roadside Resurrection." In *The Christ-Haunted Landscape: Faith and Doubt in Southern Fiction*. Susan Ketchin. Jackson: University Press of Mississippi, 1994.

Brown, Rita Mae. *Bingo*. New York: Bantam, 1988.

Butler, Jack. *Jujitsu for Christ*. New York: Penguin, 1988.

Butler, Robert Olen. "Up By Heart." *Had a Good Time: Stories from American Postcards*. New York: Grove Press, 2004.

Caldwell, Erskine. *The Journeyman*. New York: Viking Press, 1935.

———. *Tobacco Road*. New York: C. Scribner's Sons, 1932.

Campbell, Will D. *The Convention*. Atlanta: Peachtree Publishers, 1988.

Capote, Truman. *The Grass Harp*. New York: Random House, 1951.

Childress, Mark. *Crazy in Alabama*. New York: Putnam, 1993.

Clark, Martin. *Plain Heathen Mischief*. New York: Knopf, 1994.

Covington, Vicky. *Gathering Home*. New York: Simon & Schuster, 1988.

Crews, Harry. *The Gospel Singer*. New York: Morrow, 1968.

Daugharty, Janice. *Necessary Lies*. New York: Harper, 1996.

Davis, Rod. *Corina's Way*. Montgomery: NewSouth Books, 2003.

Douglas, Ellen. *A Family's Affairs*. Boston: Houghton Mifflin, 1992.

Dubus, Andre. "If They Knew Yvonne." In *Selected Stories*. New York: Vintage, 1995.

Dunn, Mark. *Welcome to Higby*. San Francisco: MacAdam/Cage, 2002.

Edgerton, Clyde. *Lunch at the Piccadilly*. Chapel Hill, NC: Algonquin, 2003.

———. *Raney*. Chapel Hill, NC: Algonquin, 1985.

———. *Where Trouble Sleeps*. Chapel Hill, NC: Algonquin, 1997.

Ellison, Ralph. *Invisible Man*. New York: Random House, 1952.

———. *Juneteenth*. Edited by John F. Callahan. New York: Random House, 1999.

Faulkner, William. *As I Lay Dying*. New York: J. Cape, H. Smith, 1930.

———. *Light in August*. New York: H. Smith & R. Haas, 1932.

———. *The Sound and the Fury*. J. Cape, H. Smith, 1929.

Flowers, Sandra Hollins. "Hope of Zion." In *The Christ-Haunted Landscape: Faith and Doubt in Southern Fiction*. Susan Ketchin. Jackson: University Press of Mississippi, 1994.

Fox, William Price. *Dixiana Moon*. New York: Viking Press, 1981.

———. "Southern Fried." In *Southern Fried Plus Six*. Philadelphia: Lippincott, 1968.

Gaines, Ernest. *In My Father's House*. New York: Knopf, 1978.

———. *A Lesson Before Dying*. New York: Knopf, 1993.

Gautreaux, Tim. "The Pine Oil Writer's Conference." In *Welding with Children*. New York: Picador, 1999.

———. "Waiting for the Evening News." In *Same Place, Same Things*. New York: St. Martin's Press, 1996.

Godwin, Gail. *Evensong*. New York: Ballantine, 1999.

———. *Father Melancholy's Daughter*. New York: Morrow, 1991.

Gurganus, Allan. *The Oldest Living Confederate Widow Tells All*. New York: Knopf, 1989.

Hampton, Lynette Hall. *Jilted by Death*. Silver Dagger Mysteries. Johnson City, TN: Overmountain Press. 2004.

Hannah, Barry. *Yonder Stands Your Orphan*. New York: Atlantic Monthly Press, 2001.

Hoffman, William. "The Question of Rain." In *By Land, by Sea*. Baton Rouge: Louisiana State University Press, 1988.

Holman, Sheri. *The Mammoth Cheese*. New York: Atlantic Monthly Press, 2003.

Hood, Mary. *Familiar Heat*. New York: Knopf, 1995.

Hurston, Zora Neale. *Jonah's Gourd Vine*. Philadelphia: Lippincott, 1934.

Inman, Robert. *Dairy Queen Days*. Boston: Little, Brown, 1997.

Jones, Madison. *The Innocent*. New York: Harcourt, Brace, 1957.

Karon, Jan. *At Home in Mitford*. Elgin, IL: Lion Publishing, 1994.

Kay, Terry. *After Eli*. Boston: Houghton Mifflin, 1981.

———. *The Year the Lights Came On.* Boston: Houghton Mifflin, 1976.

Kenan, Randall. "Ragnarok! The Day the Gods Die." In *Let the Dead Bury Their Dead and Other Stories.* San Diego: Harcourt, Brace, Jovanovich, 1992.

———. *A Visitation of Spirits.* New York: Grove Press, 1989.

Kidd, Sue Monk. *The Mermaid Chair.* New York: Viking, 2005.

———. *The Secret Life of Bees.* New York: Viking, 2002.

King, Cassandra. *The Sunday Wife.* New York: Hyperion, 2002.

Kingsolver, Barbara. *The Poisonwood Bible.* New York: HarperFlamingo, 1998.

Lee, Harper. *To Kill a Mockingbird.* Philadelphia: Lippincott, 1960.

Lester, Julius. *Do Lord Remember Me: A Novel.* New York: Holt, Rinehart & Winston, 1984.

McCullers, Carson. *Clock Without Hands.* Boston: Houghton Mifflin, 1971.

Morgan, Robert. *This Rock.* Chapel Hill, NC: Algonquin, 2001.

Morris, Michael. *A Place Called Wiregrass.* Tulsa, OK: RiverOak Publishing, 2002.

O'Conner, Flannery. "The River." In *A Good Man Is Hard to Find and Other Stories.* New York: Harcourt Brace Jovanovich, 1955, renewed 1983 by Regina O'Connor.

———. *The Violent Bear It Away.* New York: Farrar, Straus, & Cudahy, 1960.

———. *Wise Blood.* New York: Harcourt Brace, 1952.

O'Toole, John Kennedy. *The Neon Bible.* New York: Grove Press, 1989.

Patillo, Beth. *Heavens to Betsy.* Colorado Springs: WaterBrook Press, 2005.

Payne, Peggy. *Revelation.* New York: Simon & Schuster, 1988.

Pearson, T. R. *Gospel Hour.* New York: William Morrow, 1991.

Penn Warren, Robert. *All the King's Men.* New York: Harcourt, Brace, 1946.

———. "The Confession of Brother Grimes." In *The Circus in the Attic and Other Stories.* New York: Harcourt, Brace, 1975.

Percy, Walker. *Lancelot.* New York: Farrar, Straus & Giroux, 1977.

———. *Love in the Ruins.* New York: Farrar, Straus & Giroux, 1971.

———. *The Second Coming.* New York: Picador, 1980.

———. *The Thanatos Syndrome.* New York: Farrar, Straus & Giroux, 1987.

Price, Reynolds. *The Good Priest's Son.* New York: Scribner, 2005.

———. *The Tongues of Angels.* New York: Atheneum, 1990.

Reynolds, Sheri. *The Rapture of Canaan.* New York: G. P. Putnam's Sons, 1995.

Sams, Ferrol. "Widow's Mite" and "Judgment." In *The Widow's Mite and Other Stories.* Atlanta: Peachtree Publishers, 1987.

Sherman, Dayne. *Welcome to the Fallen Paradise.* San Francisco: MacAdam/Cage, 2004.

Smith, Lee. *On Agate Hill.* Chapel Hill, NC: Algonquin, 2006.

———. *Saving Grace.* New York: G. P. Putnam's Sons, 1995.

———. "Tongues of Fire." In *Me and My Baby View the Eclipse: Stories.* New York: Putnam, 1990.

Street, James H. *The Gauntlet.* Garden City, NY: Doubleday, Doran, 1945.

————. *The High Calling,* Garden City, NY: Doubleday, Doran, 1951.

Styron, William. *Lie Down in Darkness.* London: Hamish Hamilton, 1952.

Sumner, Melanie. *The School of Beauty and Charm.* Chapel Hill, NC: Algonquin, 2001.

Tartt, Donna. *The Little Friend.* New York: Knopf, 2002.

Taylor, Peter. "The Decline and Fall of the Episcopal Church." In *The Oracle at Stoneleigh Court: Stories.* New York: Knopf, 1993.

Tyler, Anne. *Saint Maybe.* New York: Random House, 1991.

Walker, Alice. *The Color Purple.* New York: Harcourt, Brace, Jovanovich, 1982.

Welty, Eudora. *Delta Wedding.* New York: Harcourt Brace, 1946.

————. *Losing Battles.* New York: Vintage Books, 1978.

————. *The Optimist's Daughter.* New York: Random House, 1972.

————. *The Ponder Heart.* New York: Harcourt, Brace, 1954.

Wilcox, James. *Modern Baptists.* Garden City, NY: Dial Press, 1983.

Wright, Richard. "Fire and Cloud" and "Down by the Riverside." In *Uncle Tom's Children.* New York: Harper, 1938.

————. *Native Son.* New York: Harper & Brothers: 1940.

Index